IS YOUR WORK RICH
AND PURPOSE-FULL?

- Do you see yourself, through your work, as making a difference in the world?

- Do you view most work days with a sense of enthusiasm?

- Have you developed your own philosophy of life and success?

- Do you feel a sense of meaning and purpose for your life?

- Are you living your life now — or hoping that life will work out someday?

Work can be more than just a job
with

THE POWER OF PURPOSE

THE
POWER
OF
PURPOSE

Richard J. Leider

FAWCETT GOLD MEDAL • NEW YORK

A Fawcett Gold Medal Book
Published by Ballantine Books
Copyright © 1985 by Richard J. Leider

Library of Congress Catalog Card Number: 85-90631

ISBN 0-449-12840-7

Manufactured in the United States of America

First Edition: July 1985

CONTENTS

Introduction

Every one of us needs a reason to get up in the morning. What's yours?

This book is about that reason. As human beings we hunger for meaning and purpose in our lives. At the very core of who we are we need to feel that our lives do make a difference. We all need a reason, a good reason, to get up in the morning. We need to feel a sense of purpose.

But where do feelings of meaning and purpose come from? How can I find them in my life?

Many of us wait. We wait for a great leader, a special moment or situation to come along and push us up the hill. We plod on.

What about you? Do you have some purpose that is outside yourself and larger than yourself?

The power to create a "purpose-full" life resides within you. Without tapping that power, you might end up with a life that hasn't even begun to be used up. If you're waiting for a great leader or organization to create meaning and dignity and purpose in your life — you might wait your whole life long.

The central principle of this book is that **the way to happiness and meaning in life is through a sense of purpose.** To be truly alive we need to focus on purpose beyond ourselves.

We need to periodically clarify the answers to questions such as these:

Who am I?

Why am I here?

What do I have to contribute that will make a difference?

What do I value and believe in? (Am I living my values?)

What need do I see that I'm moved to address?

When I use the word **purpose**, I am referring to that deepest dimension of you — your innermost self — where you have a profound sense of who you are, where you came from, where you're going, and how you might reach that point.

Our purpose starts with the acceptance of the basic truth that who we are and what we do does make a difference. It begins also with the belief that we have the power to shape the basic answers of our lives. Purpose provides meaning for life; it provides us with guidelines for answering such questions as:

Why do I get up in the morning?

Why do I go to work?

What am I doing with my life?

This book is a tool in the search for purpose. It is not another book about goal-setting. Having a sense of purpose is more than just getting to those important things we have put off doing.

Purpose is a decision and a process.

Purpose is something you live every day. It's not something to be delivered — it's to be acted upon. It's a process of directing and organizing your day-to-day life experience. Purpose means focusing on what deeply satisfies you, occupying yourself and your time with people, commitments, ideas, and challenges that help you feel worthwhile and make a difference.

A purpose often comes in unexpected forms and packages. It surprises us. It may come in the form of a still, small voice that is difficult to hear above the noise of a hectic life-style. When you accept the idea of purpose in general, you never know when in a particular situation a need is going to pop up that you can fill — right where you are — in your home, your job or organization, in your community, with your spouse or friends.

Purpose most often emerges right where you are — right in the same old circumstances you've got.

> **"In maturity, then, one undertakes commitments to something larger than the service of one's convulsive little ego! . . . religious commitments, commitments to loved ones, to the social enterprise and to the moral order. In a free society we shall never specify too closely what those commitments should be."**
>
> —John Gardner

As a career and life-planning consultant, I have worked with hundreds of people and organizations who want to make a difference. Initially, some want to make enough money so their family will be secure no matter what happens to the economy. Some want the freedom to create a full and rich life-style — to travel and buy fancy toys. Some want to be more successful than their neighbors and friends. Some want recognition and the visibility that proves their worth.

I've observed the simple truth that taking care of our own needs and wishes doesn't sustain us for long. There is still something missing. That something is the power of purpose in our lives.

I hope that you will detect and clarify your own sense of purpose — for if I have served mine — this book will be a catalyst for you. Where do you start? Read on.

Richard J. Leider
Minneapolis, Minnesota

Acknowledgments

Although I write for myself and for strangers, I do not work alone. There are other people who have inspired this book.

It began with David McNally. David coined the title of this book and it was his vision which served as a driving force for both a film and book on the subject.

Three years ago, David called me out of the blue to propose the idea of a book to accompany a film he was producing. The film, *The Power of Purpose*, was inspired by a young Canadian, Terry Fox. Terry Fox had lost a leg to cancer at the age of eighteen. Two years later Terry had run halfway across Canada to raise money for the Canadian Cancer Society. David, at a low point in his own life, happened to pick up a book about Terry Fox's life. The Fox story moved him to clarify his own purposes and to approach his own future more boldly. David's magnificent obsession became a mission to guide others in finding the power of purpose in their own lives.

David called me to write the book. On the phone, I told him of how I had happened to meet Terry Fox while camping with my family in Canada. Click . . . ! David hung up the phone on me! A few minutes later he called back, apologizing and saying, "I was so shaken that I couldn't speak." He went on. "To think that of all the people I might have called to discuss this project with, it happened to be you — a person who had also been moved by Terry Fox. It was just too much. The feelings overwhelmed me!"

Despite numerous obstacles in producing the film, David persevered. Days, months, went by, and he always said the same thing — "This story has got to be told!" He was refreshingly sensible and imaginative in his approach toward the project. With wit and unfailing good nature, he became a lifelong friend. He is a model not only for me, but for all readers of this book.

Section I

THE BIRTH OF PURPOSE

Chapter 1

PURPOSE BEGINS
WITH CLARITY

"This is the true joy in life, the being used for a purpose recognized by yourself as a mighty one; the being thoroughly worn out before you are thrown on the scrap heap; the being a force of Nature instead of a feverish selfish little clod of ailments and grievances complaining that the world will not devote itself to making you happy."

—George Bernard Shaw

Inspiring words from George Bernard Shaw, but how easy it would be to dismiss them as having no meaning for us.

And yet, most of us want to know that there is a purpose to life—that our being here does mean something—that what we do does make a difference.

Most of us are interested in purpose and meaning in our lives. However, we generally become deeply concerned about it only when some event forces us to pay attention—an illness, a death, a problem with a relationship, a major economic change, a loss of job, etc. We take life for granted until an event wakes us up and forces us to ask, "What am I doing with my life?" Then we attend to clarifying our real values. The most effective life-style, however, results from a conscious decision to live purposefully before we face a triggering event.

Purpose begins with clarity. Clarity simply means that we have a specific image of what we want. Most of us don't even have that. Instead, we have specific images of what we don't want. Holding on to images of what we don't want leaves us powerless. We end up spending most of our lives trying to avoid what we don't want!

Clarity about what we want is a prerequisite for purpose. Most people who get what they want begin with, or develop along the way, a very clear picture of what they want.

The way to spend your time and energy wisely is to clarify the goals and purposes for which you live and then order your life accordingly.

"If you don't know where you're going, any road will get you there." Unfortunately, most of us are only vaguely aware of the beliefs and values that guide our day-to-day decision-making. Only in times of crisis do our values become clear. Then we become aware of what's important in life and worth spending time on. "What specifically is it that I want?" "Why am I doing this?" "What do I want to accomplish?" "What kind of person do I want to be?" "What do I want my experiences to be?" The purpose of this questioning is to clarify what you want.

It's difficult to feel the same clarity of purpose in the busyness of daily life. Yet, this is the first step. We must ask ourselves what our busyness is all about.

One of the chief requisites for a fully alive life is purpose! The only constants in the lives of people who enjoy inner peace are a clarity of the principles they live by and an active purpose beyond themselves. We need at our very core to experience ourselves positively. We need evidence to believe we are good people and growing or becoming better. Clarifying what we want out of life helps us to satisfy that basic need to believe **I matter**, that **my life does make a difference**.

For her book, *Pathfinders*, Gail Sheehy interviewed hundreds of people who were recommended to her as models of success. One key question separated the bona fide pathfinders from the others: "Are you devoted to some purpose or cause outside of yourself and larger than yourself?" While most responded, "NO," the true pathfinders answered that question, "YES!" True success comes when life makes sense to people. Commitment to a purpose larger than ourselves gives us that meaning.

> **"Pathfinders with a purpose are not heroic statue material looking down their holy noses at the grubs who are all the rest of us. Many are people who say: 'This neighborhood (or city, school, church, country) is going to the dogs. It's my responsibility to make it better.' Most commonly such people find a purpose— or respond when it finds them—at the local level . . ."**
>
> —Gail Sheehy

Purpose brings a feeling of empowerment. It is based on the assumption: "There is always something I can do. And, from something, something comes. Because I make a difference!"

If you search for happiness as an end in itself—you'll never find it. Affluent society has given many of us the means to happiness, but often we still cannot see the end, a purpose to live for. More people have more time and money to spend, but nothing meaningful on which to spend them.

You don't have to wait for a crisis in order to clarify and direct your life through purpose-full choices. Throughout this book are many exercises called *REFLECTIONS*. Start right now with Reflection #1 below. Use these exercises to reflect on your life purposes.

REFLECTION #1

Look ahead.
How would you like to celebrate your eightieth birthday? Imagine you're about to celebrate it. As you look back on your life, what would you like to be able to say as to how your life **made a difference**? If you could throw a log on a fire each time your life really made a difference, be it a small act of courage or kindness, or a work of art, would you have a bonfire or a flicker?

(continued)

5

Write a statement about how your life has **made a difference**:
My eightieth birthday—"**Here is a person who** . . .

REFLECTION #2

How old do you think you will live to be?
_____age   _____year
What should I do with the remaining time so that I can
look back over my life with no regrets?

REFLECTION #3

My current purpose in life is:

All variations in purpose have in common the devotion
to **discovering what is needed and wanted and then producing it—during this lifetime!**

Chapter 2

THE FIVE MAJOR INGREDIENTS OF PURPOSE

There are five major ingredients that form the foundation for living with a sense of purpose:

1. Purpose provides meaning for our lives.
2. Purpose serves as a principle around which to organize our lives.
3. Purpose rallies our strengths around that which deeply satisfies us.
4. Purpose clarifies our interests and our work.
5. Purpose often comes in unexpected forms and packages.

Purpose is that deepest dimension in you—your innermost self—where you have a profound sense of who you are, where you came from, where you're going, and how you might reach that point.

Purpose is not a noun. It's never a static condition we can preserve. Purpose is a verb, a process we engage in over and over again. It's a process we live every day. It's not something to be delivered—it's to be acted upon. It's a process for directing and organizing our life experience.

It's tempting to ignore the dimension of purpose in life, since the consequences of our neglect usually don't show up until crisis points. Thus, we spend most of our primary energy building a life-style, making a living, and becoming successful.

When you scratch under the surface of your drive for success, what's there? Why do you get up in the morning?

Commitment to something larger than our own success gives life meaning. To what are you committed? What are you going to do with your success once you get it? What's the bottom line of all your effort? These questions lead us to the other side of purpose. What purposes larger than yourself are you focusing on?

Your sacrifice for your children?

Your wish to make the world a better place for them to live?

Your wish to make a difference in one person's life each day?

Your sense of responsibility to your employees? Your customers or clients?

Your loyalty to your friends?

These are tough questions. Purpose is demanding. Let's look closely at the five major ingredients of purpose.

1. Purpose Provides Meaning For Our Lives

Having purpose in our lives means that something (an aim, a goal, an interest, a person, an idea) attracts us enough to move us to action on its behalf and is important enough so that focusing on it orders our activities and provides our lives with a sense of meaning. Purpose helps me in understanding what is relevant to my life, what it is I live for, who I am and what I am about in actual day-to-day living. My world makes some sense to me.

Living on purpose is living the meaning of my life. I am steadied and whole in my living, and the various situations of day-to-day living are more easily handled. Such a unifying sense of direction can withstand much stress and is actually strengthened by overcoming difficulties.

Ben, a friend of mine, was running in a local 10K weekend race where there were a number of wheelchair athletes.

Post-race conversation led Ben to an awareness of the obstacles they faced in their normal day-to-day activities. Soon he explored the realities of wheelchair life at the college he was attending and at his mother's office. He began writing letters and lobbying the administration to provide funds for greater accessibility for handicapped students. Ben went on to study special education and now consults with organizations on making their buildings more accessible to people with physical disabilities. A purpose-full career began with a 10Km race and today testifies to what Ben's values are.

Through purpose, I am more responsive to myself, just as an artist is more in touch with himself when absorbed in the needs of a painting. There is a selflessness that goes with being absorbed in something you genuinely find interesting; yet it is a sense of being **more** yourself.

We are growth-seeking creatures. Purpose is necessary for our very health and survival. If you doubt this, check out the rates of illness and death when people lose or give up their growth or sense of purpose. People who retire without something to retire to have a much higher incidence of mortality and illness than those who have a focus.

Why is this? Is it natural aging? I think not. Work provides an ongoing sense of direction.

Purpose gives us reasons for being and doing. And, as if by magic, life returns the favor by being fuller, richer, and longer.

At an American university, when sixty students were asked why they had attempted suicide, 85% said the reason had been that "life seemed meaningless." More important, however, was that 93% of these students suffering from the apparent lack of purpose in their lives, were socially active, achieving academically, and on good terms with their family situation.

"This happens in the midst of affluent societies and in the midst of welfare states! For too long we have been dreaming a dream from which we are now waking up: the dream that if we just improve the socio-

9

economic situation of people, everything will be okay, people will become happy. The truth is that as the struggle for survival has subsided, the question has emerged: survival for what? Ever more people today have the means to live, but no meaning to live for."

—Viktor Frankl

We cannot have deep and enduring satisfaction unless we have self-esteem. We cannot have self-esteem unless our lives are an earnest attempt to express the finest and most enduring values which we are able to appreciate. Therefore, purpose is an important condition for an enduring satisfaction with life.

Through finding and helping to develop my purpose, I discover and create the meaning of my life. And in acting on my purpose, I live the meaning of my life. I realize the point of my life, what it is I am up to.

2. Purpose Serves As A Principle Around Which to Organize Our Lives

Most of us are starved for coherence in our lives.

Purpose can serve as a vehicle for focusing our time, effort, and ideas. The most effective people know how to carry out daily activities while keeping their eye on a longer-range principle or set of values. John F. Kennedy set a goal in 1960 to place a person on the moon by 1970. It captured the **power of purpose** of an entire nation. Ideas were generated by the thousands with the result that a seeming science-fiction dream became a reality in ten years.

Purpose has a way of ordering values and activities around itself; that is the real power behind the purpose! It might even involve redesigning our life-style and work-style in order to bring out our talents and full potential.

When we come to care for some other person or are moved by something, many things previously felt to be important fade in significance. If our purpose is genuine enough, it involves us deeply and orders all areas of our life. We begin to eliminate what is irrelevant and what is so much clutter. A simplification takes place and we achieve a clarity as to what we're about. We don't need to pretend to be what we're not. What is of real importance stands out more clearly.

Purpose can tolerate conflicts in priority; there will be times when this priority rather than that one comes first. But such conflicts even out in the long run. We really cannot be devoted to many things at the same time.

> **"Voluntary simplicity involves both inner and outer condition. It means singleness of purpose, sincerity and honesty within, as well as avoidance of exterior clutter, of many possessions irrelevant to the chief purpose of life. It means an ordering and guiding of our energy and our desires, a partial restraint in some directions in order to secure greater abundance of life in other directions. It involves a deliberate organization of life for a purpose."**
>
> —Richard Gregg

The way to spend your time and energy wisely is to know the goals and purposes for which you live and then to order your life accordingly.

Kay and Brad Englund know this ordering process well. Several years ago they took a year off to travel around the world. When they returned, they chose to become vegetarians (for health reasons and on principle). Having observed that so much of the world goes to bed hungry, they decided to eat more lowly on the food chain. They live by that decision every day. Many relatives and friends don't understand it. Entertaining and meal preparation are more complicated. Does their commitment to that principle make a difference? Will it influence others? There are no guarantees.

A prime requirement for opening yourself up to a sense

of purpose may be your willingness to voluntarily choose a simpler pattern of living. Purpose unfolds as you challenge your present life-style.

In what ways is your life unnecessarily complicated? In what way could you improve your life by simplifying it?

In the context of our lives, purpose has a way of ordering our activities and life-style around it. When this ordering is honest, there is a basic stability in our lives; we are in sync with the world instead of merely drifting. The power of purpose focuses our energies and rallies our strengths.

3. Purpose Rallies Our Strengths Around That Which Deeply Satisfies Us

If my purpose is important enough to give meaning and order to my life, it must also rally my strengths and talents. I must be able to make use of my particular skills.

Through purpose I come to a truer appreciation of my strengths, as well as my limitations, and I can take pride in the successful use of my strengths.

Purpose enables me to be complete, just as painting enables the artist to be himself. Through my talents, purpose becomes active and alive in my life rather than merely professed. Purpose is not ready-made; it must be shaped and clarified through my acting on it.

Purpose means using your skills on what deeply satisfies you. Occupying yourself and your time with people, commitments, and challenges that help you feel worthwhile means rallying your most enjoyed skills.

We cannot force a particular purpose to be more important than it is, just as we cannot force ourselves to be genuinely interested in something. The way to know the true depth of some purpose is to begin it! Through applying our skills and strengths, we help to both create purpose and discover it. Confidence and security come only with the fullest use of our distinctive talents.

Purpose is possible only in the present. It is something you live every day. The problem is always how to respond to a person, idea, ideal in the here and now; we must always work with what we have and from where we are. An artist's vision of the completed work can only function in the present. Confidence and security come only with the fullest use of our distinctive talents.

Ten years ago a close friend, Rolf, asked me "Are you having any fun—you know—enjoying your life?"

Actually, I had been asking myself that same question—but conveniently not listening or paying attention to my own response.

In answering my friend, I said, "Things are okay. I believe what I'm doing is making a contribution —you know—doing something worthwhile. But no, I don't feel like I'm really enjoying my life. In fact, I feel as though I'm waiting for something to happen—for something to move me one way or another!"

The speed of my response surprised me. Strangely, I had not been thinking of personal enjoyment. Work was work. I began reflecting on my friend's question. It gradually became clear to me that even if I was doing a worthwhile thing—I was a bank human relations officer—if I was not enjoying it, something was wrong. Perhaps it was not the best use of my gifts, talents, or abilities.

Wanting to understand why I seemed to be feeling more struggle than joy, I began to see my delusion—that "work is work and not to be enjoyed."

The discovery of this simple principle, by which I had been living my life, led to a whole cascade of insights about the role of work and purpose in my life.

As I began acting on these insights, prompted by the question of a friend and found through further reflection, I began to experience more and more of the joy that had been eluding me. My principle became, "No one should be deprived of joy in one's work and life!"

How about you?

REFLECTION #4

Are you having any fun—enjoying your work and your life—at this age or stage?

[   ]   Yes
[   ]   No
[   ]   ?

Do you feel that your major work activity makes a contribution (e.g., is needed and wanted and can best be served by your talents)?

[   ]   Definitely yes
[   ]   Most of the time
[   ]   Some of the time
[   ]   Definitely no

Are you devoted to some principle or purpose outside yourself and larger than yourself?

[   ]   No
[   ]   Yes (specify):_____
_____

If you are not devoted to some purpose or cause outside yourself, what is the reason for this?

[   ]   Haven't found one that engages me.
[   ]   Too busy at this stage of my life.
[   ]   Have been frustrated or disappointed by purposes or causes to which I was once devoted.
[   ]   Have no interest in a purpose or cause.
[   ]   Not applicable; I have a sense of purpose.
[   ]   Other:_____
_____

Activities that derive from purpose are not a burden forced on us; there is a harmony between what we feel we are supposed to do and what we want to do. Through purpose we grow by becoming more honest with ourselves and more aware of our strengths which naturally motivate us.

Honesty is present in realizing that my particular purpose is not in any way privileged. What is really important is not whether my purpose is more important than your purpose, but that we be able to have something to care for.

True purpose means overcoming the arrogance that exaggerates my own talents at the expense of yours. I am able to present myself as I am without self-display; I don't need to pretend to be what I am not. There is nothing for others to see through. My purpose rings true. There is not a significant gap between how I act and what I really feel. I am living my values.

4. Purpose Clarifies Our Interests And Our Work

Are you bored with life or do you lack energy and vitality?

These conditions often occur because we don't have a dream worth dreaming—a dream worthy of our talents and highest ideals. Often it's because our interests are vague, meager, or nonexistent.

Boredom is often based on one simple belief: "There's really nothing I can do." And from nothing, nothing comes.

Sometimes people feel frustrated. "If only I could care for someone or something," they say, implying they are not satisfied because they do not feel needed, but would be if they had something to serve.

The United States and many other developed nations seem to be in a period of social drift. They appear to be losing a sense of purpose and direction. Many people seem to be waiting for a leader or a significant event to make clear the nature of a new vision. The uncertainty and growing restlessness have prompted a new willingness to think the unthinkable, to seriously consider what life means and where we wish to go. There is reason to think that the kind of power fostered by a sense of purpose is especially appropriate in our times and circumstances.

A sense of urgency seems to derive from the many serious societal problems, including: the prospects of a chronic energy shortage; growing terrorist activities worldwide; growing demands of less developed nations for a more equitable share of the world's resources; the prospect that we may poison ourselves to death with environmental pollutants; growing voting apathy; a changing balance of global power given rapid nuclear proliferation; climatic changes which may induce periodic but massive famine in certain areas; chronic fiscal crises in many of our largest cities; chronic unemployment and underemployment; challenge to the legitimacy of leaders in nearly all major institutions; and so on. These are but a few of the many issues which make the **power of purpose** an appropriate response to a pressing situation. Our needs as individuals uniquely match the needs of our society.

The activist cares for this cause, the writer cares for that idea, the parent cares for this child, the citizen cares for that community issue, and so on. Purpose means investing yourself in something that moves you, even if it is laboring to put bread on the table. It means living inside the question, "Why am I here?" It means that you're able to say, "I'm useful. My life makes a difference."

Transforming your interests into action is the key to purpose. It's easy to say that you value world peace; it's tougher to march or sit in protest against defense monitoring activities. It's tougher, but more rewarding, when you back up your principles with action. There are numerous ways to get action. The trick is to find the cause that moves you and the role that fits your most enjoyed skills.

Polly Edmunds did not set out to become a crusader. Until age 40, she was a wife, parent, and special education administrator with little public visibility. She first learned about the nuclear arms race through her church and then from a friend who was forming a group called "Women Against Military Madness" (WAMM). What she learned appalled her. She asked herself, "What am I doing that makes a difference? How do I start working on the nuclear arms issue?" She took the first small steps to make a difference in her world. As she matured, so did her commitment. She saw that risk-taking was going to be an essential element of her commitment. She's been arrested as a peace demonstrator and has spent time in jail. She's an active leader in WAMM. She started with simple day-to-day choices and discovered a sense of purpose and commitment which she expresses in some way each day of the year.

What about you? What needs doing in your world? Where are you committing yourself and your resources?

Purpose clarifies a direction for our growth and behavior. It gives our life meaning and a frame of reference. Because of our purpose, we know why we get up in the morning. Our purpose serves as the glue which holds the various aspects of our life together. It gives our life greater consistency and predictability. It serves as an inner guide by which we can judge appropriate responses to events, people, places, and things.

Purpose is the principle or inner vision that shapes our day-to-day activities—our habitual outlook.

5. Purpose Often Comes In Unexpected Forms And Packages

When you commit yourself to the idea of purpose in general, you never know when in a particular situation a need is going to pop up that moves you. Purpose often comes in unexpected forms and packages. It often comes in the form of a still, small voice that is only faintly heard above the noise of a hectic life-style.

There are many things existing in our world that we don't see because we are not looking for them or perhaps because we don't feel capable of making a difference with them. **The world we see tends to be the world we look for.**

Show two people the same painting and each will see a different aspect; we each will find what we are predisposed to look for. In a small Maasai village in Tanzania last year, one person with whom I was traveling saw a depressing, run-down dung hut. Another saw a graceful, friendly, and beautiful group of people. The same scene gave one person an idea for a story. Another, his eye on the trail ahead, saw nothing.

The world presents to each of us that which we seek.

There is not a community or area that does not offer abundant opportunity for purpose to every person living there.

Purpose starts with discovering what is needed and wanted and producing it right where you are!

Victor Hugo wrote, "Nothing in this world is so powerful as an idea whose time has come." Yet, it's a funny thing about people and their ideas. Most of the time the idea is the only thing they're willing to risk.

There has never been a monopoly on getting good ideas; but the number of people who are moved by an idea, who will **risk taking a stand** on an idea, is small indeed.

I believe that the most fortunate people on earth are those who have found an idea that's bigger than they are—that moves them and fills their lives with constant interest, aliveness, and struggle—and who go from one purpose to another all their lives.

If you find yourself running out of ideas, in which you have an interest, complete the following exercise.

REFLECTION #5

Get a copy of today's newspaper. Read every page—the editorials, features, sports, ads, entertainment, community, and world events. As you read, ask yourself, "What needs doing?" Underline all the issues you detect.

List twenty-five needs you saw in your paper.

Circle the one or two interests that move you, about which you feel, "Someone really ought to do something!"

While running the risk of over-simplifying, I think that it can be said that we are unhappy to the extent that we fail to give of ourselves to others.

This puts purpose, aliveness, and peace of mind within reach of everyone.

The concept of purpose is not an end point but a process. It is not a description of the last days of your life, but of its continuing saga from this moment on, into a future as you would have it be if you could determine it. And you can!

Much that is important about the human condition cannot be explained by these five major ingredients, but they may help us to better understand our own lives.

Chapter 3

WHY WAIT FOR A CRISIS?

Purpose in life is not invented by ourselves. Rather, it is detected.

"... we can discover this meaning in life in three different ways; (1) by doing a deed; (2) by experiencing a value; and (3) by suffering."

—Viktor Frankl

It is often in the midst of #3 above—suffering—that we pull back from the entanglements of daily survival and ask the basic questions such as:

- What is the meaning of my life now?
- What is my purpose in living?
- Where am I headed?
- How can I be happy?

The result of a crisis is often the letting go of petty concerns, conflicts, and quests for greed, and the realization that life is short and every moment precious.

But why wait for a crisis?

Cancer therapists Carl and Stephanie Simonton give their patients this advice:

"You must stop and reassess your priorities and values. You must be willing to be yourself, not what people want you to be because you think that is the only way you can get love. You can no longer be

dishonest. You are now at a point where, if you truly want to live, you have to be who you are."

Could there be any better advice for us?

Whenever we are confronted with an inescapable situation (e.g., cancer) or a fate which is unavoidable, then we are given a last chance to express our highest value, to fulfill our deepest purpose. What matters is the attitude we take toward crisis and suffering.

Terry Fox is a clear example. For this young Canadian, the necessity to reflect on the meaning of life was thrust upon him early in life. Two days after his eighteenth birthday, Terry learned he had a cancerous tumor in his right knee. His leg would have to be amputated immediately, since the cancer could spread through the rest of his body. Now, suddenly, life was tentative, no longer to be taken for granted. Despite the shock and the speed with which Terry's life had changed, he spent little time in the trap of self-pity. Within the confines of his hospital room, Terry detected a purpose, his personal reason to live.

Many of us will be forced to reflect upon the reason for our existence when we experience severe crises.

"But you don't have to do like I did—wait until you lose a leg or get some awful disease—before you can take the time to find out what kind of stuff you're made of. Start now. Anybody can."

—Terry Fox

Two weeks after his surgery Terry began chemotherapy. The cancer clinic and the painful treatments were a reminder to Terry that almost half of all cancer patients never recover. Terry could no longer take his life for granted. He decided he wanted to do something for the people who were still there. He began to detect what it was he cared deeply about; what moved him. Terry began to find a purpose.

"Somewhere the hurting must stop and I'm prepared to take myself to the limit for the cause."

—Terry Fox

His purpose was to run all the way across Canada to raise one million dollars to fight cancer. He would give his money to the Canadian Cancer Society.

A sense of purpose is never handed to us. We get it by deciding to have it. We get it by deciding that, yes, I matter. A sense of purpose starts from within and only we know if we have it. Only we know if there is something in our life that makes us want to get up in the morning.

One purpose in life is not more important than another. There is purpose whenever we respond to something we believe in.

On September 1, 1981, after running three-fifths of the way across Canada, Terry Fox had to leave his Marathon of Hope. The **power of purpose** had transformed an average athlete into a person who, with an artificial leg, ran a marathon a day for five months! He never finished. The cancer had spread to his lungs.

By the time of his death in June, 1982, he had raised over twenty-four million dollars and had inspired thousands of people.

Terry Fox had a direct impact on my own life. Before reading about him or starting this book, I saw him "on the run" in Ontario. While camping with my family around the perimeter of Lake Superior during the summer of 1981, we came upon Terry Fox running the hills along the lake just outside of Thunder Bay, Ontario. Sandwiched in between the flashing red lights of a highway patrol car and the van with a "Marathon of Hope" banner on its side, was Terry Fox—with a look in his eyes that is etched indelibly in my memory. That look of determination was **the power of purpose** in action.

He challenged me with that look. He made me ask— "What am I doing with my life?" "Am I willing to pay a price?" "Am I willing to make a commitment?"

Ever since I was a kid I've had an intense curiosity about what motivates people. I've always felt convinced that there could be more to my life if only I could find it. Tempted by the glowing promises of self-help books, I read them all, and they all said, "The first step is to decide what your *aim* is in life."

So I sat down cheerfully one day with pencil in hand to jot down my aim. It didn't come!

The self-help books had suggested that I should want some definite achievement (e.g., to be promoted, to earn so much money, to get something done). But none of these aims moved me.

I was unable to find that clear aim which it was said would bring me fulfillment. I was beginning to question whether there might not be something wrong with me.

Whenever I managed to commit myself to a goal, I found I achieved more than I ever expected, but the results never brought me the measure of fulfillment promised by the books.

I had never been able to find, in one of these goals, a central focus for my life. On one day, a certain goal would be important; on another day, a different goal would capture my fancy. I had never committed myself to anything wholeheartedly.

Terry Fox got me thinking again. I started to realize that I needed an aim—a purpose or a principle by which I could deliberately guide my daily life. I wasn't clear about what principles did guide my life.

I began to shape a new vision for my life; not the shaping of goals to fit some preconceived purpose, but the gradual detecting and clarifying of a purpose—something which could grow out of the essence of my particular talents and interests. I realized that I couldn't really fail at being myself!

Each of us is the steward of his particular talents. Once we detect and focus our gifts, our strengths—we, too, can surpass our expectations.

Terry Fox symbolized what most of us want to know—that there is purpose to life, that our being here does mean something, that what we do does make a difference.

The sheer determination of one individual can turn a seemingly mediocre idea into a smashing success. Behind the creation of any great deed is at least one individual who was consumed by a driving force to make a difference. The only place you or anyone else can find this kind of motivation is within.

Caution!

In describing people like Terry Fox who have detected a sense of purpose, I feel a certain uneasiness. I don't want to be describing an unrealistic do-gooder ideal. Purpose had always meant to me do-goodism. It had always meant being dull and burdensome; it meant missing things, shutting spontaneity out of my life.

Terry Fox changed all that. He evidenced the aliveness and intensity I sought for my own life. He was awake! He was the actor (not the spectator) brought to mind by Zorba the Greek:

"Life is trouble. Only death is not. To be alive is to undo your belt and look for trouble!"

It is not what deeds we do that give us a sense of purpose, but knowing why we do them. Having a sense of purpose is far different from being a do-gooder.

Do-gooders merely use people and activities as opportunities for ego recognition. As a result, they often keep score of their deeds. People with a sense of purpose learn to move the focus of their attention and concern from themselves to others. They have learned the joy of transcending purely self-directed concern.

"Let life question you!" Dr. Viktor Frankl suggests that an openness to being questioned by life is a way to find a sense of purpose—to find out who we are. He suggests that most of us are questioning life, rather than letting it question us. We ask:

What has life done for me?

Will things go my way today?

What's in it for me?

Most of us question life in this way. However, there is a more profound wisdom in reversing the questioning and **letting life question us**.

Try going through a day reversing the questioning process. Consistent joy in life and work means reorienting our questioning.

Work, play, relationships, learning, and service to others are all part of a full life. Consider **reorienting your questioning** over the next week...

These questions are to be judged only by you. Only you can answer them or reorient them.

FROM QUESTIONING LIFE	→	TO LIFE QUESTIONING YOU
1. *Work*: "How can I get a raise or a promotion around here?"	→	"What needs doing around here and what can I do to produce it?"
2. *Play*: "I wonder if this party will be boring?"	→	"What will I do to make this party more interesting?"
3. *Relationships*: "Why doesn't she ever listen to me?"	→	"How effectively can I listen to her today?"
4. *Learning*: "Why didn't the instructor explain that in more detail?"	→	"How can I help the instructor understand my needs more clearly?"
5. *Service*: "When will this church board shape up?"	→	"What does this board need and how can I produce it?"

Chapter 4

THE RUSTOUT
SYNDROME

We need tensions. In fact, we search for tensions. Today, however, we often do not find the right kinds of tensions. That is why we sometimes create them.

It goes without saying that we should not be subjected to too much tension. Rather, what we need is a sound amount—of the right kind. Not only too-great demands, but also the opposite—the lack of challenges—may cause disease.

Even Hans Selye, the father of the stress concept, admitted that "stress is the salt of life."

What we need is a specific tension—between a person and a meaning he or she wants to fulfill. We are not just in search of tensions per se, but in particular, in search of tasks whose completion might add meaning to our lives. Today, however, many of us are not finding such a meaning and purpose. Psychotherapists and counselors report that a major complaint they hear day in and day out is a feeling of futility and emptiness. Its main symptom is boredom!

Pervasive boredom is an attitude toward life held by many people today. Take for example the vice-president of a high-technology company that I consult with. "I just can't seem to get going," the vice-president said. "I used to be an up-and-coming salesman with this company. Now I can't get interested in what I'm supposed to do. I know I should get rolling. I'm sleepwalking through the day. And I'm awake at night. I'm going to the liquor store twice a week. Once used to be enough. I feel trapped!"

In short, he had **rusted out**. He felt trapped in a kind of vocational quicksand. He was not challenged. He felt he could not leave; nor could he succeed.

He went on to say, "I don't know how much longer I can last in this job. I've been with the company for fifteen years and have changed jobs every two to three years. The organization charts keep changing, but the politics don't. We're still being told what we must do and when. The old virtues of initiative and taking risks are not being rewarded. The system process of rewards is more political now. I'm demoralized."

What was happening to this executive? He felt that no one cared about the contribution he was making. That caused him to raise the question "What for?"—as if he'd lost sight of his purpose for living.

Graham Greene writes, in *A Burnt-Out Case*:

> "'Self-expression is a hard and selfish thing. It eats everything, even the self. At the end you find you haven't even got a self to express. I have no interest in anything anymore, doctor. I don't want to sleep with a woman nor design a building.'
>
> 'Have you no children?'
>
> 'I once had; but they disappeared into the world a long time ago. We haven't kept in touch. Self-expression eats the father in you, too.'
>
> 'So you thought you could just come and die here?'
>
> 'Yes. That was in my mind. But chiefly I wanted to be in an empty place, where no new building or woman would remind me that there was a time when I was alive, with a vocation and a capacity to love— if it was love.'"

Most people probably experience **rustout** at some point in their lives.

If a person is not challenged by meaningful tasks and is spared the positive tension surrounding such tasks, **rustout** occurs. It is the condition of not using your talents and abilities toward some end you feel is needed and wanted.

Rustout is similar to a garden in which nothing grows—it's empty. Life lacks purpose; nothing moves us. There is nothing to explore that might open us to our own aliveness. Our work lacks promise; life continues day-by-day at the same petty pace. Helen Keller said, **"Life is either a daring adventure or nothing."** Rustout is when life has become the latter. We experience life as a scorecard in which we are more concerned about how we compare with others—whether they are ahead or behind us—than using our talents on something that truly interests us. We sold our souls to the grade-givers. We have become hypnotized by old norms and loyalties.

Like generalized stress, rustout cuts across all ages and levels. People in these situations feel chronic fatigue, anger, self-criticism, and indifference. They can no longer invest themselves in others or in their work.

William James said, **"Compared with what we ought to be, we are only half awake."** Everyone knows the phenomenon of being more or less awake on different days. In the **rustout syndrome**, our talents are slumbering and the interests of the day do not call forth our energies.

We need to wake up to our potential for higher forms of purpose. But how can we awaken? How can we escape this sleep? **Do we need a periodic <u>wake-up call?</u>** We usually do not wake up by ourselves. It often takes another person, more awake than ourselves, to give us a periodic wake-up call. Without a person like this, we often need a major crisis to get our attention.

REFLECTION #6

Who awakens you? Who gives you that periodic <u>wake-up call</u> to the possibility that your life is?

Jot their name(s) below:
- _____
- _____
- _____

Affluent society has given many of us the means, but we cannot see an end—a meaning to live for. More people have more time to spend but nothing purposeful on which to spend it. Despite an almost universal belief to the contrary, the pursuit of happiness as it is interpreted today is a myth. Ease, comfort, and a state of having arrived (i.e., achieved one's goals) do not constitute happiness for most human beings. We have tried it and we know better!

The fact is that life is either hard and satisfying or easy and unsatisfying. A life without challenge and difficulty leads to a sparse and shallow existence. Comfort and leisure are just not enough. If this were the case, the large number of Americans who enjoy relative affluence would be ecstatically happy!

The true story of happiness involves striving toward meaningful goals—goals that relate a person to a larger context of purposes. Challenge helps us focus on the widest questions of our being. It's a deepener.

So, if society offers us too little of the right kind of tension, we start creating it—the very tension we have been spared. We deliberately place demands on ourselves by voluntarily exposing ourselves to stress situations, if only temporarily.

Many would argue that helping or expressing good will toward others provides a sense of positive stress. Hans Selye has suggested that the way to enjoy a rewarding life-style, free of disabling stress, is to practice "altruistic egoism." In essence, this involves helping others and earning their love while at the same time recognizing our own needs and enhancing our own self-esteem.

Selye points out that our biological nature drives us toward self-preservation or what might commonly be called selfishness. Selye's line of thought suggests that only by linking this self-centered innate nature with an attitude of earning the goodwill and respect of others through altruistic efforts, will a happy, meaningful life result.

We may never fully understand our altruistic urge, let alone human nature, but the heart of purpose may be centered in the simple idea of helping our fellow human beings (and ourselves, in the process).

We can choose to make our love for each other what our lives are all about. The challenge is for us to find what provides that feeling that **we make a difference**. For most of us, purpose is at the heart of this search.

To explain purpose adequately, we must look to a deeper underlying vision. It is an old vision but an enduring one that is reexamined in every era. The nature of this vision is summed up well by the historian, Arnold Toynbee, in his *Study of History* (Vol. III):

> **"These religious founders [Jesus, Buddha, Lao Tse, Saint Francis of Assisi] disagreed with each other in their pictures of what is the nature of the universe, the nature of spiritual life, the nature of ultimate spiritual reality. But they all agreed in their ethical precepts. They all agreed that the pursuit of material wealth is a wrong aim. . . . They all spoke in favor of unselfishness and of love for other people as the key to happiness and to success in human affairs."**

Section II

LIVING ON
PURPOSE

Chapter 5

WHY DO YOU GET UP IN THE MORNING?

Many of us say we don't have enough time to take care of our lives and careers. Then before we know it, we're right! It's easy to get so busy living your life that you don't have time to notice it.

One of the things most visible in our society is that many people are very busy doing many, many things, often with enormous intensity. If you look more closely, you realize that, in a way, they are busy trying to find recognition for their worth. We do many things in order to answer the question, "Am I worth being?" Busyness is a way of gaining approval for our self-worth. Busyness is also a status symbol. But it is a nervous way of living because we continuously seek approval from outside ourselves and then end up saying, "We are what we do!"

William Least Heat Moon wrote in *Blue Highways*:

"He had retired from his job as a school custodian and lived now on Social Security, a Marine disability pension, and another from the school system. He worked at the museum for the occupation of it.

'I never worried about making a living,' he said, 'but I've done thinking about making a life. It's hard to know the difference sometimes, and it must be getting harder, judging by all them that don't know the difference now.'

What is the difference?

'Best way to tell it is that if you're trying to make a killing, what's going to get killed is your life.'"

Stop for a moment and reflect on the quality of your life. Are you feeling satisfied? Challenged? At peace? Fully alive? Healthy? Do you have what you want to have? Do you give what you want to give?

REFLECTION #7

Answering small questions could be a good way to look at some of the small things that fill your life. You might find your own answers interesting and not what you'd expect. Tell the truth.

- When did you have a good time singing?
- When did you see the sunrise?
- Who do you miss?
- What has a child told you lately?
- When did you teach someone something that made a difference?
- When did you do something you'd never done in your life?
- What would be a good question for someone to ask you?

Share your list with a friend.

Recently, many of us have come to acknowledge publicly what we privately knew all along. Namely, that by successfully surviving adolescence and early adulthood, we did not ensure ourselves of a tranquil, jolt-free passage through the rest of our lives and careers. We change; our priorities and values shift; confidence grows, dissolves into doubt, then back again; relationships evolve; careers and life-styles become static or take on new meanings. Forming a complex web of life patterns, we're either growing or stagnating, building or slipping.

We saw *The Big Chill*, the movie about sixties' people living in the eighties, the campus radicals who had turned down their idealistic passion and become successful: a lawyer, a gossip journalist, a manufacturer of running shoes, and a TV star. Yet they were all somewhat uneasy about their apolitical lives. They, like most of us, periodically face a swath of difficult questions:

- Who am I?
- Is my public self different from my private self?
- Are other people my age asking the same questions I am?
- How can I make my life more alive?
- Which risks make sense for me to take in order to keep growing and feeling alive?
- Which values, beliefs, and commitments do I most cherish?

Every year from podiums, hundreds of commencement speakers exhort graduates to make commitments, to believe in something, to change the world, to create a life that balances public and private ideals and pleasures. The speakers know something about the conflicts between the ideal and the real, work and pleasure, public and private life.

REFLECTION #8

A Commencement Address

You have accepted an invitation to make a short commencement address at a local high school or college. What do you say to eighteen to twenty-one-year-olds in our society? The only thing they have in common is that every one of them wants to succeed as a human being in his or her own way. What would you say to them? Outline below a fifteen-minute speech to deliver to such young people. Share what you have learned, what you know is right and will work and will result in satisfaction and accomplishment.

Every human being—based simply on being human—periodically wonders, "Who am I?" Most religions—Buddhism, Hinduism, Christianity, or Islam—deal with this question. We have to struggle to find our true self. If we act on a false self—the self that is put together by a mask of busyness—we will always jump from one illusion to another. We will never be deeply satisfied.

We need to start unmasking our illusions. Slowly, we need to discover what part of busyness is just cultural consensus (i.e., norms we accept) and what part is an expression of our real values, talents, and interests.

We're often unaware of why we're uneasy or discontent. We're like train passengers who don't know where the train is now or where it's going. Often we're surprised at where it travels and where it stops, but we stay on for the ride. Achieving a clearer vision for our lives often requires that we reroute ourselves—change our direction or destination or prepare ourselves for unexpected stops and detours. We don't have to be locked onto one track if we don't want to be; there are switches we can throw all through life.

For many of us, reflection is as tough as it is inevitable. Ideally, we should not let a day pass without spending some time revitalizing the spiritual in us. Eventually, we really listen to our deepest self; and there is an enormous hunger for that.

For every person who summons up the energy and courage to explore the quality of his or her life, there are many who hope that more busyness will feed their hunger, who plod on—waiting. Waiting for some special person or event to point the way. Waiting, perhaps, to be discovered.

A good place to start with your quality-of-life exploration is at the roots with the question, "Why do *I* get up in the morning?" (Repeat the question several times out loud.) Ask yourself what you really need in your life? A real need is something you must have to survive. After your basic needs are clear, begin to look at your wants. Wants enrich the quality of our lives. What we want reflects our values.

<u>Clarifying our values is essential to identifying a sense of purpose.</u>

Psychologist Abraham Maslow arranged human needs into a hierarchy. He claimed that our basic needs must be at least minimally fulfilled before we can move toward our wants. Our physiological needs (e.g. air, food, shelter) are the most basic. These needs must be satisfied before we can free our energies to pursue needs at the next level and so on. As Gandhi said, **"Even God cannot talk to a hungry man except in terms of bread."**

At the next level, according to Maslow, we must feel minimally safe and secure in our day-to-day activities. We all define safety and security in different ways. Our fundamental need to feel that our life and our work are rooted in solid ground is essential. In support of this, the government sponsored report, *Work in America*, cited a fifteen-year study that found the strongest predictor of longevity was work satisfaction.

At the next level we must feel a sense of companionship and affection. We need love—some kind of recognition that we have worth, that someone cares. Our self-worth can be badly damaged by lack of real or imagined love. Self-worth will rise if you engage in life and work activities that you believe are worthwhile (e.g. needed and wanted), in which you can be a contributing member of society. To the extent that you spend your precious time currency in activities that you don't value (consider "worth-less") your self-worth will diminish.

As Maslow stated,

"Even if all these needs are satisfied, we may still often (if not always) expect that a new discontent and restlessness will soon develop unless the individual is doing what he is fitted for. A musician must make music, an artist must paint, a poet must write if he is to be ultimately at peace with himself. What a man can be, he must be. This need we call self-actualization."

37

At the highest level, we operate with purpose. At this level we are growing, stretching, and utilizing our highest capabilities and talents. We are tapping **the power of purpose**.

Chapter 6

Motivation and Productivity

THE ALIVENESS INVENTORY

Each of us is located somewhere on the journey to purpose or self-actualization. Each in his or her own way must journey to seek real purpose in life. Exploring your quality of life, your sense of aliveness, will help you become more conscious of your journey—more aware of your uniqueness. There is no other human being on earth with your particular blend of needs and wants or with your unique vision for happiness. You must monitor your quality of life as you go about developing a sense of life purpose. The clearer you are about your needs and wants, the more clarity and focus you will bring to detecting your life purpose.

REFLECTION #9

What are the current signs that indicate your life is rich, full, and alive? What are the signs that indicate, no, your life isn't as full and vital as you might wish? Think of taking this inventory as you would a periodic **physical examination**. Check either Yes or No according to how you feel about each question **today**.

THE ALIVENESS INVENTORY

	Yes	No
1. Are my work life, personal life, and family life in balance?	_____	_____

(continued)

	Yes	No
2. Do I regularly enjoy hearty belly laughs?	———	———
3. Do I have written goals for my life?	———	———
4. Do I take time daily to be alone?	———	———
5. Do I have at least two nutritious people in my life?	———	———
6. Do I take time for the maintenance of good health and vitality?	———	———
7. Do I have a spiritual base and meaning in my life?	———	———
8. Do I recognize my gifts, talents and abilities, and use them fully?	———	———
9. Am I committed to a purpose?	———	———
10. Is my leisure/play activity satisfying to me?	———	———
11. Do I view life's events as opportunities to grow?	———	———
12. Do I have an effective system of daily self-management?	———	———
13. Am I an effective listener?	———	———
14. Do I take the risks necessary to live the life I have imagined for myself?	———	———
15. Do I have models for the way I'd like to be?	———	———
Total *Yes* Responses =	———	

How to Interpret Your Score

The total of *Yes* responses on the Aliveness Inventory provides a general idea of your quality of life. Compare your total score with The Power of Purpose standards:

12-15	Excellent	Your habits are enhancing your quality of life.
7-11	Average	You're obviously trying, but there are several areas open to improvement.
Below 7	Poor	Your quality of life is probably diminished by your habits.

As you reflect on your quality of life, focus on the questions you need to pay more attention to. In the following discussion, decide whether you want to take action to modify your habits. No one has all these factors going for him all the time. Everyone experiences self-doubts and ups and downs. Aliveness does not mean perfection! It does mean a willingness to live life openly and fully, acknowledging your humanness. Remember to give yourself credit where you've done well.

The Aliveness Inventory is an opportunity to reflect. Take some time right now, after your initial scoring, to reflect further about each of the questions.

Question #1: Are My Work Life, Personal Life, and Family Life in Balance?

This question is not trying to claim that there is some "ideal balance" for all people. Each of us must decide what the proper formula is for his or her life. However, it is important to understand that we do tend to define our lives by what we do. For example, the first question people often ask is, "What do you do?" and through your answer they compare themselves with you. This gives them a frame of reference to continue (or discontinue) the discussion. Work is important to our identity. It is dangerous, however, to claim all of our self-worth through our vocation, title, or business card.

We have two currencies to spend in life—time and money.

Money can be spent and re-earned; we can lose all of our savings or our business and then come back again and take another shot at it. Time, however, is the **currency of life**. And, how we spend it reflects what we truly value. Once we have spent it, it is gone—forever! It cannot be re-earned. So as you look at the first question, ponder this thought: **"If you are what you do, when you don't you aren't!"**

Question #2: Do I Regularly Enjoy Hearty Belly Laughs?

We have gotten so serious in our culture! We have forgotten how to laugh and be joyous. In fact, it is estimated that one out of three people will probably need assistance to work their way out of some kind of depression within their lifetime.

While this question uses the term "belly laughs", it really refers to **playfulness**. Playfulness is a frame of mind.

There is a direct connection between playfulness and health. If a negative mind can make the body sick, then what can make it well? Obviously, positive thoughts, such as playfulness and humor. Play is a primary need in life. Set yourself a goal to have one good belly laugh per day. When you start looking for humor in your life, you will often find it. A perspective of playfulness is increasingly important as we move through stressful events. Think of **hearty belly laughs** as internal jogging and ponder this: **"He or she who laughs . . . lasts!"**

Question #3: Do I Have Written Goals for My Life?

If you had two hundred years to live, you might not have to do much planning. However, all of us must look at the fact that we have only so many years to live. Thus, we must order our priorities accordingly. Often the trickiest part of getting what we want out of life is "figuring out what it is we want." When you ask people, "What do you want out of life?" it often boils down to two things: intimacy and options. Jot down two things that you "always dreamed of doing before you die."

- _____
- _____

As Henry David Thoreau said, **"If a man advances confidently in the direction of his dreams to live the life he has imagined, he will meet with a success unexpected in common hours."** The first step is having a dream worth dreaming!

Question #4: Do I Take Time Daily to be Alone?

This question came from a variety of sources, one of which is the Outward Bound Wilderness Schools where the **solo**—a time alone (one to three days)—is a part of the program. Many people are frightened by the solo before they begin it. After they return, however, many think that the solo was the highlight of their entire adventure. You don't have to go to the wilderness to take a solo; you can take a mini-solo of ten to fifteen minutes each day.

Since busyness is a status symbol in our society, even our leisure time is heavily scheduled. All of this busyness leads to noisy minds and keeps us from knowing our feelings and inner self. We need to make a daily appointment with ourselves—a solo—to make sure that we are paying attention to what's important in our lives. As Pascal said, **"All men's miseries derive from not being able to sit quietly in a room alone."**

Question #5: Do I Have at Least Two Nutritious People in My Life?

We all are forced to deal with **toxic** people in our lives—people who make us feel worse after we are with them than if we had not been with them at all. To offset this, we need **nutritious** people in our lives. Nutritious people have two primary characteristics: (1) their face lights up when you come in the room and (2) they have few (i.e., no) plans for your improvement.

We all need a good support network in the world we are living in today, and nutritious people need to be part of our networks. Take a minute right now and jot down the names of the four most **nutritious** people in your life.

- _____
- _____
- _____
- _____

Question #6: Do I Take Time for the Maintenance of Good Health and Vitality?

The idea behind the Aliveness Inventory is that "you don't have to be sick to get better." This certainly holds true for our health and vitality. We need to learn to pay attention to our bodily signals which tell us how we are doing and how we are feeling. We pay the price either now or later, as far as our health goes.

Aristotle's advice was sound when he said, "Be a good animal first." We need to pay attention to our aerobic capacity, flexibility, strength, relaxation, nutrition, and sleep patterns, as well as to our life philosophies and purposes.

Question #7: Do I Have a Spiritual Base and Meaning in My Life?

We need to pay attention in our lives to the "imponderables"—our spiritual base. Even Einstein, for all of his scientific wisdom, came to the conclusion, **"I cannot believe that God plays dice with the cosmos."**

Throughout our lives, we all deal with three "hungers": (1) the hunger for meaning, for leaving footprints, and for having our lives recognized as worthwhile; (2) the hunger for intimacy and community; to be cared about, and to give and receive love; and (3) the hunger for self: to grow, to understand our uniqueness, and to figure out how to most effectively use our talents during our short lifetime.

Question #8: Do I Recognize My Gifts, Talents, and Abilities, and Use Them Fully?

The words **gifts and talents** are often used to explain why we can't do something. "I don't have the talent for that." "I wish I were half as talented as you!" Richard Bach in his book, *Illusions*, says; **"Argue for your limitations and sure enough, they're yours."** What he is saying, I believe, is that we are very good at arguing for our limitations; we are not quite as effective, however, in communicating our strengths.

Most careers are made, NOT born. And that means understanding our talents and strengths and using them fully.

One forty-year study of life patterns showed that people who were dissatisfied with their occupations had an average of three to five more major health problems during a forty-year period than those who were satisfied. Many of us are miscast for what we are doing. I've observed that about fifty percent of my clients entered the occupation they did because it happened to be convenient or was an immediate economic necessity, and not because they'd really analyzed their strengths and motivating interests!

No occupation has a corner on fulfillment. We do know that the motivation to use one's talents is the power behind purpose.

Question #9: Do I Have Commitment to a Purpose?

Purpose does not mean winning the Nobel Prize or creating world-shaking inventions, life-saving exploits or artistic triumphs, or even raising twenty-four million dollars for cancer, as Terry Fox did. The simple truth is that we all need to feel significant.

Gandhi's life is an obvious example of living on purpose. This remarkable man changed the world. The world laughed when he set out to free India and her millions from the yoke of British colonialism; but that's precisely what he did. And isn't it interesting that the people who truly change the world often have no armies and nuclear weapons to help them.

Question #10: Is My Leisure/Play Time Satisfying to Me?

Often we treat ourselves like machines that need refueling, rather than as living beings who have natural rhythms of our own. The notion here of **play** indicates a frame of mind for doing something "just for the sake of doing it" (not to achieve anything)! Children know how to do something naturally essential to good mental health (e.g., play). Many of us need to relearn how to "play." Jot down five ways you really have "fun."

- _____
- _____
- _____
- _____
- _____

Then, jot down the date you last engaged in each of these five things:

How true for you is Woody Allen's thought: **"Most of the time I don't have much fun. The rest of the time I don't have any fun at all."**

Try one new play activity a month (over the next three months) just for the fun of it!

Question #11: Do I View Life's Events as Opportunities to Grow?

The key to happiness and inner peace in one's life is not an absence of crises. "Well, what is it then?" The key is a better coping system for dealing with the inevitable crises of life. Throughout our lives there are crossroads or events that are opportunities for us to grow. Often we live as if someday there will be no such events and that life will be a nice "calm harbor." The calm harbor is a myth! Sure, there are plateaus in our lives, but we are generally dealing with some kind of change. As Jonas Salk said, **"Life is an error-making and an error-correcting process."**

We often say to ourselves "If only I had such and such, I'd be happy." The reality is when we work too hard, we want rest; when we rest too much, we want work; when we are with too many people, we want solitude; when we have too much solitude, we want companionship. Bachelors often envy happily married life-styles; married people envy bachelor life-styles; young envy old and old envy young, etc., etc.... Discontent comes with the territory—with being human!

How do you cope with life's ups and downs? Do you view them as opportunities to grow?

Question #12: Do I Have an Effective System of Daily Self-Management?

Many of us have systems that we use at work for managing our responsibilities, objectives, etc. How well do you manage your life on a day-to-day basis?

An airline pilot usually goes through a checklist just before takeoff and just before landing. We need the same sort of system—a checklist to keep ourselves in touch with our life priorities. What system do you use to pay attention to your important relationships, your health and your spiritual life?

Suzuki has suggested: **"I'm an artist at living and my work of art is my life."** Managing one's time currency with an effective system of self-management is essential in today's environment. Balancing work and relationships is one of the major stressors today. Contrary to many people's thinking, to be organized often means the liberation of time and energy, not the cramping of our style.

Question #13: Am I an Effective Listener?

Often a client has said to me: **"You are the first person I have ever been completely honest with!"**

With whom are you really honest? Who really listens to you? To whom do you really listen?

Listening is one of the lost arts in our culture. The best relationships, which we all seek, are usually built, like a fine lacquer finish, with the accumulated layers of many acts of listening. We are all starving to be heard!

I advise my clients to make periodic getaways—weekly or monthly—just to listen to the people they care about. Do you have at least one three-hour block of togetherness time every two weeks? Or, at least one getaway weekend every three months?

As Ralph Waldo Emerson said: **"Rings and jewels are not gifts but apologies for gifts. The only gift is a portion**

of thyself." The greatest gift you can give is to <u>listen to</u>
<u>somebody today</u>!

Question #14: Do I Take the Risks Necessary to Live the Life I Have Imagined for Myself?

Jot down one **risk** that you have taken in the last six
months:

_____

_____

_____

Risk has sex appeal. We all want to feel as if we're
risking. Risk makes us feel intensely alive. However, the
natural companion of creative action and risk is fear. Fear
lets you know you're on the right track; that what you're
doing is big enough for you. When you start moving, you
start shaking.

Question #15: Do I Have Models for the Way I Would Like to Be?

Terry Fox is a model for me. My father is a model. Zorba
the Greek is a model. I don't want to be Terry Fox or my
father or Zorba. However, there is something in each of
them that brings out the best in me, that nudges me toward
living my values or acting on my priorities and purposes.
Identify, in the space below, those people who are models
for your vision of your life.

_____

_____

_____

_____

Mark Twain said: **"Few things are harder to put up
with than the annoyance of a good example."** I disagree.

Models, looked at appropriately, fuel my vision of the possibilities in my own life.

People who answered yes to most of the questions on the Aliveness Inventory are not paragons of virtue. The fact is that they are just as concerned with inner achievements as outer achievements. They are people who have made decisions about their values, their goals, their relationships, etc. They come from a place inside themselves to define who they are and who they will be. Aliveness can only be self-measured. In fact, others may not even notice, because aliveness is not a superior state of being—it's an attitude. If you have done the work of reflecting and risk-taking that this Inventory measures—congratulations! You are in a distinct minority.

The majority of the people who take the Inventory fall in the middle range (7–11 Yes answers). They're pretty comfortable with some areas of their life and they haven't done much at all with others. What this boils down to is that there are basically only two motivational systems: **avoiding the negative** and **pursuing the possible.** This book is clearly about pursuing the possible. Scores in the middle range indicate a combination of avoiding the negative and pursuing the possible. Remember that we are talking about an attitude, something that is quite hard to measure.

A low score (below 7) generally points to one of two characteristics: (1) people who are generally avoiding the negative in terms of most issues in their lives; or (2) people who may be going through a general overhaul or reassessment of their lives, who thus come up with many question marks on the Inventory. If you scored low you might consider seeking a support group or seeking professional counsel on some of the issues raised.

As you review the Aliveness Inventory in the context of examining the total quality of your life, keep in mind that having purpose in life starts with a clear answer to the question, "Why do I get up in the morning?"

Chapter 7

LIVING YOUR VALUES

How many people do you know who can truthfully say that they live, for the most part, the way they really want to live? Can you say that you do?

It has become popular for people to talk about their own values and about value systems. Probably less than ten people out of a hundred, however, have really examined their lives and the values that determine their day-to-day behavior.

Living your values means living consciously. The ability to clarify your values and to commit energy to them means having a definite approach to your life.

What values are most important at this stage of your life? Which of your values do you consciously live?

We live in a dynamic environment. Job requirements, relationships, organizations, and economics will be different tomorrow from what they are today and we are often reminded that it is no longer possible to settle into a totally predictable pattern for a lifetime. But clarifying or periodically assessing what we value helps us choose a definite approach to life — a quality of life that we have defined for ourselves. How many people do you know who drift with their circumstances, accepting less than life has to offer and taking no risks to create a definite approach to life?

A value is a thing or condition which you consistently act on to get or to keep.

Thus, the more consistently and energetically you commit resources (time and money) to something, the more you value it. This means that <u>you can get a pretty clear idea of your values by observing the way you spend your two most valuable currencies—time and money.</u>

Some people might delude themselves with statements about their values. They might say, "Family comes number one in my life!" Yet, if asked what they do, have done, or plan to do with family, they might have trouble coming up with an answer. Talk about values has very little to do with living your values. Values are identified by what you *do*, not by what you say. We live our values when we "walk our talk."

We really have two types of values. You can think of your **touchstone** values as those things or conditions you say you want. Our touchstone values represent our excellence—our image of ourselves at our ideal, genuine best. You can think of your **daily** values as those things or conditions you actually do take action to get or keep. All of us have **touchstone** values—things we want to do or be "some day." We have more possibilities than we'll ever have time to pursue.

The most important measure of our values, however, lies in the relative balance of **touchstone** and **daily** values; the extent to which your day-to-day behavior represents values of your own choosing. Living our values means consciously choosing a definite approach to our lives and acting on our approach on a day-to-day basis.

To live our values means to become more honestly aware of ourselves and to live in closer harmony with our beliefs. Value clarification helps develop our ability to make decisions about our life purpose. Through living our values, we learn what it means to have integrity.

The following exercise highlights some of the most commonly discussed **touchstone** values. Any attempt to provide an exhaustive listing of possible values would not serve our purposes well here. But, these categories merit a close look.

REFLECTION #10

TOUCHSTONE VALUES

Listed below are twenty key areas of life. Key areas or broad categories which you might consider indicative of your primary touchstone values. You'll probably want to add others to suit your own purposes.

In Column A, rank from 1 to 10 (1 = highest priority), the things or conditions *you say you want*—your **touchstones.**

In Column B, rank from 1 to 10 (1 = highest priority), the things or conditions *you actually spend the majority of your time* (and money) to get or keep on a day-to-day basis—your **daily** values.

How closely does "B" align with "A"? Do you "walk your talk?"

A My Touchstone Values	B My Daily Values	
( )	( )	Achievement (sense of accomplishment)
( )	( )	Work (paying my own way)
( )	( )	Adventure (exploration, risks, excitement)
( )	( )	Personal Freedom (independence, making own choices)
( )	( )	Authenticity (being frank and genuinely myself)
( )	( )	Expertness (being good at something important to me)
( )	( )	Service (contribute to satisfaction of others)
( )	( )	Leadership (having influence and authority)
( )	( )	Money (plenty of money for things I want)
( )	( )	Spirituality (meaning to life, religious belief)
( )	( )	Physical Health (attractiveness and vitality)

(continued)

A My Touchstone Values	B My Daily Values	
( )	( )	Emotional Health (ability to handle inner conflict)
( )	( )	Meaningful Work (relevant and purposeful job)
( )	( )	Affection (warmth, caring, giving and receiving love)
( )	( )	Pleasure (enjoyment, satisfaction, fun)
( )	( )	Wisdom (maturity, understanding, insight)
( )	( )	Family (happy and congenial living situation)
( )	( )	Recognition (being well known, prestige)
( )	( )	Security (having a secure and stable future)
( )	( )	Self-Growth (continuing exploration and development)

Would your spouse or closest friend see you as someone who holds the touchstone values checked?
_____Yes _____No   Why or why not? _____
_____
_____

Deciding which are our most important values is not easy. One of the difficulties is overcoming societal and family pressures to accept certain values as our own.

A value may seem to be a relatively vague concept. But, by reminding yourself of it on a day-to-day basis, you will refine it into a clear and practical principle that you can carry out.

A framework of values is at the very heart of our decision-making process; without it, we lose confidence in our decisions. We don't feel sure about our choices. Decisions made on the basis of personal values tend to be made with more commitment than those based on purely situational factors.

Commitment to clearly stated values leads to living those values. There are several factors that make living our values difficult:

1. *Fear of failure*—without values and ideals we can never fail. Making a commitment to a value involves risks to one's self-esteem if the value is not adhered to.
2. *Lack of self-awareness*—it is difficult to live our values if we are not certain about who we are and what our priorities are.
3. *Responsibility and choice*—to live our values implies a sense of responsibility and a choice within our environment. To become committed to a value we must feel empowered to choose among options in our life. It means choosing those things you'd like to pay more attention to and letting go of those you want to stop "servicing."
4. *Lack of knowledge about the world*—an important part of values is the concept of choosing them freely from among several options. Being knowledgeable about one's options will help to clarify one's goals.

Any desire to make changes in your life or work can be met with a hundred reasons why it might not work. Most such questions can only be answered by trying it . . . risking it . . . living life as an experiment! One experiment is worth a hundred "buts."

REFLECTION #11

Look over your touchstone and daily values. Are you living them? What obstacles are getting in your way? Below are thirty-five ideas for leading a simpler life. Sometimes through simplifying our life-style we can create more time to live our values. Check the areas you have an interest in experimenting with. Decide to set your own priorities about your use of time, money, space, and energy!

_____Play the Income Game. Figure out how you could live on half your present income. Would you have to change your life-style in any way? Would the differences in life-style and values help you to meet your real priorities?

(continued)

_____Turn off the TV and begin playing games again. (Don't forget reading books, storytelling, and playing musical instruments.)

_____Avoid unnecessary auto travel. (Most people will drive their cars to a destination more than two blocks away.)

_____Shop carefully. Make a list. Plan your shopping for three days.

_____Share the car. Buy a bicycle. Walk more. Begin to use public transportation. People's inability to enjoy time (rather than "killing" it) causes them to rush everywhere in cars.

_____Reserve a place for quiet . . . a place to take your daily "solo." Respect the value of silence.

_____Unplug the phone.

_____Educate yourself about your body. To simplify your life, you must know how to stay healthy and to heal yourself once you get sick.

_____Cultivate your friendships. Stay at home and engage in honest conversation and express your affection for others.

_____Reclaim your creativity. Make your own gifts, recipes, stories, etc. Create your own celebrations.

_____Get up earlier. (Practice "mind over mattress.")

_____Make an inventory of the clothes you own. Which ones have you worn in the last year? Might your unused clothing be given, traded, or sold to others? Do you tend to shop for clothes when you're bored or need an ego boost? What else could you do to feel better?

_____Organize the closets better.

_____Decorate your home simply. Home decorations are an expression of one's life-style.

_____Eliminate unnecessary appliances. (The average household has twenty-nine electrical appliances.) Share tools and appliances with others.

_____Try to avoid the nonreturnable. (We discard forty billion throwaway bottles a year.) Recycle newspapers, metal cans, etc.

_____Find out about free events. Check out the weekend newspapers for listings.

_____Rediscover your community. Exploring different neighborhoods is fascinating and educational.

_____Take off on a trip one weekend with no map and no plans.

_____Re-vision your goals and dreams. Make a list of what you would like to do in your lifetime. Please dream!

_____Re-evaluate your job. Ask yourself what relation your present job has to your real hopes for yourself.

_____Re-evaluate your debts. Determine how much your present job and life-style are tied up to installment payments, maintenance costs, and the expectations of others.

_____Develop flexible hours for study, job sharing, income sharing, and other innovations.

_____Discuss how you feel today about Ralph Waldo Emerson's spiritual and practical plan for "plain living and high thinking."

_____Look over your check register or receipts for the last twelve months. Are your patterns of consumption basically satisfying, or do you buy much that serves no real need? (Note: living simply need not be equated with living cheaply.)

_____Reflect upon the impact of your consumption patterns on other people and on the earth.

_____Simplicity requires living with balance. To find such balance in your daily life requires that you understand the difference between your "needs" and your "wants." Make a budget of those things that are essential to your survival and growth . . . your "needs."

_____Seek an integration of the ways you work, play, live, and do, rather than simply using one to make another possible.

_____Stop during the day to become aware of the way you are breathing. Take time out for deep breathing several times a day.

_____Have occasional family meetings where everyone is encouraged to talk about how things are working.

_____Practice saying "NO" to people without feeling guilty.

(continued)

One of the deepest urges in life is to grow. Trees burst through the soil, cocoons emerge into butterflies, babies become adolescents. We must grow and fulfill our changing needs if we are to feel vital and fully alive. The happiest people are those who have had the courage to grow and risk in response to their values.

 ## RISKS

To laugh is to risk appearing the fool.
To weep is to risk appearing sentimental.
To reach out for another is to risk involvement.
To expose feelings is to risk exposing your true self.
To place your ideas, your dreams before a crowd is
      to risk their loss.
To love is to risk not being loved in return.
To live is to risk dying.
To hope is to risk despair.
To try is to risk failure.
But risks must be taken because the greatest hazard
      in life is to risk nothing.
The person who risks nothing does nothing, has
      nothing and is nothing.
They may avoid suffering and sorrow but they
      cannot learn, feel, change, grow, or live.
Chained by their certitudes they are a slave; they
      have forfeited their freedom.
Only a person who risks is free.

—Anonymous

Chapter 8

BRINGING YOUR LIFE
INTO BALANCE

Is your current vision of success the same one you held ten years ago?

Success and money may be part of a **better** life, but they do not ensure happiness in that life. As the saying goes, "There are two ways to be rich; one is to have more, the other is to want less." If there is any doubt about this, look at those who retire with full pockets only to die of what doctors are almost willing to call a "broken heart."

The way each of us defines success and values money can tell us nearly all there is to know about us! This is perhaps not a new observation. Yet an understanding of our attitudes toward success is an important part of life purpose and is an area open to all of us to explore.

How often do you hear (or say), "If we just had enough money, then we could—" Marriage counselors tell us that conflicts about money rank near the top of the issues they see constantly in troubled marriages.

Most of us work to get something. We are willing to do a job, work long hours, and endure much stress if it will let us accumulate enough money to buy a new house, get more sports equipment, etc. Yet it often turns out that money and possessions which go with making lots of money impose responsibilities and restrictions that inhibit our freedom. In fact, possessions are often amassed in order to help us feel better about ourselves.

Success is a mirage. It disappears just as we arrive at the

point where we were convinced it would be. Our definition of success keeps shifting as we age.

Before age forty, socially accepted values often dictate our success. Then, as Carl Jung, Daniel Levinson, and other life-style researchers point out, during the "second half" of life, people often detach themselves from public definitions of success in favor of ones that are more personal and meaningful.

Success implies **arrival**. Arrival, however, makes us want a new or different destination! What matters in terms of success is keeping alive to what you want and need right now! Not what you said you wanted ten years ago, and not what society defines as success for you. You are in a position to detect your own inner definition of what success is.

With respect to the ability to see through the manipulation, advertising, phoney social values, and other forms of societally defined success, Ernest Hemingway accurately coined the blunt term "crap detecting." He believed that a good writer needs "a built-in, shock-proof crap detector." With regard to success, we all need one too!

Of course, most people will keep running after external success, believing that this will satisfy the internal hunger. It never will.

The evidence all around us is that an increasing number of people feel that the pendulum has swung too far beyond a certain level of income. They would prefer to define their success as a better balance, a middle path. They prefer to devote more time to other areas: personal (growth, education, creative expression, etc.), household (gardening, home-building, child care, etc.), and community (volunteer social services, performing arts, simple human contact, church, politics, etc.). To have balance in your life means getting worthwhile results in a variety of areas, all of which add up to your definition of success and quality of life.

When you bring your life into balance, you don't focus your whole life on one thing or one pursuit or one source of satisfaction. You develop a **full quality of life.**

Many people tend to focus their energies on the work or

career area, getting great rewards there, but often neglecting other areas which could greatly enrich their lives. Eventually the other areas shrivel up and become barren and unrewarding.

Think of life at three levels—the **having** level, the **doing** level and the **being** level.

Having is the state of experiencing the benefits of money, security, status, etc. It is the ability to build our life systems and survive as responsible human beings.

Doing is activity; it stems from the day-to-day flow of events and demands. It is how we spend our time in accomplishing tasks, achieving goals and making things happen for ourselves and others.

Being is the basic experience of being alive and whole. It is the experience we have when we are "living our values," and when we are "on automatic" because of our commitment to a purpose. It is the experience we have in deep prayer or meditation, the experience of being clear and at ease with oneself. To be a human being means to *be*—to be fully awake and conscious of choosing a definite approach to our lives and acting on our approach on a day-to-day basis.

The three elements fit into a cycle. The most important measure of our quality-of-life lies in the relative balance of needs in the Having-Doing-Being Circle; the extent to which our day-to-day energies are spent pursuing one or another of these needs.

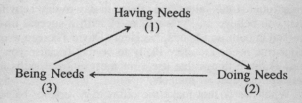

A prevailing attitude in our society is this: If I *have* enough (possessions, money, security, etc.) that will allow me the options to *do* more of what I want (have time, work options, leisure, etc.), and, if I'm doing what I want, I will *be* happier (have joy, inner peace, etc.). In theory it looks good. The only trouble is that it is not working for a great number of people.

Our **having** needs seem to be insatiable. And they keep changing. In a world characterized by inflation and change, we are constantly reminded by many sources including the media of what we need to "have" to be happy and up-to-date. Success is like a mirage. We arrive only to see another destination. We finally have our dream house only to see another. Happiness is always "out there."

The way it actually works is to *reverse* the cycle.

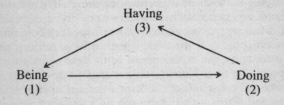

You must first *be* who you are (clarify your deepest values, talents, nature, etc.). That clarity will point the way to what you might *do* with your time and energy (how to live your values), in order to *have* what you want. If you are engaging your **touchstone** values and talents in day-to-day activities that you believe in, **"you will meet with a success unexpected in common hours,"** as Henry David Thoreau wrote. Your true needs are more likely to be met because you do best at those things that use your most enjoyed skills and reflect your deepest hungers.

When we do not make the effort to reverse or balance the Having-Doing-Being Cycle, we block the talents, energy, and integrity that give life its vitality. We may slip through our entire lives without ever experiencing the deep satisfaction that comes from "being thoroughly used." When some of us die, our tombstone will probably read—"Here lies (your name)—his/her potential fully intact!"

Through balance we gain an understanding of the basic purpose of life, and experience the joy of making good use of our talents and interests, and shall have a tombstone that reads, "Here lies (your name)—his/her potential thoroughly used up!"

The truth is that many of us have lost the sense of what it means to "be"—to celebrate each day. Why look primarily to the future for happiness, when we can learn to celebrate every moment of our lives?

Consider what happens when we think only of the future goals of having. A few years ago, with several others, I ventured into a dream to build a restaurant. This restaurant would have a special feel to the way service was rendered. We decided to build it in Vail, Colorado. We began the project filled with enthusiasm. Things went smoothly enough, but then one day a serious problem came up. The restaurant was costing thousands of dollars more than we had projected. (Does this sound familiar?) We became discouraged. The energy from dreaming about the completed place was waning. We decided to keep on building, getting ever more deeply involved. As more problems arose, we found our dreams further fading. Finishing the restaurant was frustrating! It was taking too long and it was much more costly than we thought it would be. We struggled further, and opened up. But eventually, as obstacles continued to arise, we decided to give up, to sell the dream restaurant, and turn our attention elsewhere.

The "having" dreams about our future success were far more wonderful than the "being" reality. Has this happened to you? How often? When we reach our goal, we often find it is only a brief success, a high that quickly passes. Yet we were willing to trade months of tension, unhappiness, and anxiety for a few moments of fleeting success.

When we believe that success will come only when we reach our **having**-goals, when we fail to celebrate each day with balance, we cut ourselves off from the true joy of life.

We need a balance for our energies, to support us when the inevitable day-to-day difficulties arise. Don't sell your life to your having-goals.

We live in a world that moves very fast and pressures us to keep up. Most of us do not want to live this way, but we get caught up in the demands for approval society places on our lives in the "rat race." On the surface we may appear happy, but inside we suffer from the tensions imposed by this rapid pace. We move so fast that our opportunities for self-expression diminish. We become so used to the pace that as we grow older we do not have time to appreciate ourselves; our natural ideas and feelings are discouraged; we grow out of touch with our senses; we no longer know what we truly feel; we become strangers to ourselves.

How can we rediscover the secret of enjoying each experience we undertake?

Stop! Look carefully at how you live and work. Look at how you keep from enjoying your life and work. Listen to the little voice inside you—your inner signals.

Try this. . . .

REFLECTION #12

Choose a simple task to complete. Do one task only. Devote *all* your attention to what you are doing. Be aware of each detail involved. Focus your attention on that one task until you are finished. Focus your attention with a playful, enjoyable quality. Then take on another task and continue the process. You will find your clarity and purpose deepen and become a natural part of whatever you do. **Mindfulness** is the combination of awareness, clarity, and purpose brought to bear on even the smallest details of experience. As you become skilled at being **mindful**, you become aware of the motivation underlying your actions. The awareness you gain in this way gives you control over the direction and purpose of your life.

"A few years ago I met an old professor at the University of Notre Dame. Looking back on his long life of teaching, he said with a funny twinkle in his eyes: 'I have always been complaining that my work was constantly interrupted, until I slowly discovered that my interruptions were my work.'"

—Henri J. M. Nouwen

Remember, there are two currencies that make up our quality of life: time and money. Time is the real currency of life. While money can be spent, lost, or squandered, and then earned again, time cannot be re-earned. It will eventually run out. Life will end. Opportunities will be gone in the "wink of an eye."

We give no thought to time's value—usually because we lack a clear sense of life purpose. Believing "there's always time," we postpone things for the future, spending our valuable currency in the form of boredom and postponements.

We hurry to finish one thing, and leap into another task before the first is finished, moving so fast that there is little time for true appreciation.

Learning to use time well requires organization and balance. We need to learn to proceed carefully, step-by-step, fully using and appreciating each experience before moving on to the next.

Accounting for all your time forces you to develop more awareness of how you're "spending your life." When you learn to "spend" your time more carefully, time itself seems to expand and to hold more value. We come to structure our lives with more clarity, and the expression, "having a good time," means something.

REFLECTION #13

Keep track of how you use each hour today:

A.M.		P.M.	
6:00	_____	6:00	_____
7:00	_____	7:00	_____
8:00	_____	8:00	_____
9:00	_____	9:00	_____
10:00	_____	10:00	_____
11:00	_____	11:00	_____
12:00	_____	12:00	_____
1:00	_____	1:00	_____
2:00	_____	2:00	_____
3:00	_____	3:00	_____
4:00	_____	4:00	_____
5:00	_____	5:00	_____

Section III

WORKING ON PURPOSE

Chapter 9

DAILY BREAD AND DAILY PURPOSE

What are your expectations of work? Is work something to be suffered through and endured? Or is work synonymous with growth or an activity to be enjoyed?

After ten years as a consultant to American business organizations, I have come to the conclusion that most people perceive work in one of two ways: (1) they are devoted to work only as a means to a materialistic end such as career advancement; or (2) they have a sense of purpose that is inconsistent with the purpose of the organization for whom they work. In short, most people do not like their jobs very much. And judging by the dramatic rise in the number of stress-related problems among workers at all levels, many of us feel alienated from any meaning in our work.

But we press on, blind to what it is that we're after. Toward what end do so many strive? The work ethic is obviously not dead or even dying. Michael Maccoby in *The Gamesman* saw it as the advancement of our own careers. We will make tremendous sacrifices for it, will bend over backward to avoid "making waves" to advance it, and will treat ourselves as objects to be "packaged" and "marketed" to further it. The consequence of such an orientation to work, according to Maccoby, is that we begin to view life and work as a game; to become motivated primarily by competition, winning, and achievements, and to begin valuing shallow emotional attachments, both at home and at work. Since most organizations are designed to function as money-generating machines, the result is an employee population with highly refined skills of the head, but not of the heart.

There is good evidence that a growing segment of the work force desires greater significance in their work. Many of us are tired of working for organizations that grind us down and offer money and status in return for stressful and unfulfilling lives. This feeling extends, I have observed, across all levels of organizations.

Daniel Yankelovich observed that people all over the country are reconsidering the relative merits of conventional objects of success, such as advancement, and are beginning to place higher value on more personally satisfying achievements, such as closeness to self, family, community, and nature. Such people are beginning to pursue an "ethic of commitment" in which they give more to society than they take from it.

Much of my work with people and organizations involves helping them become clearer about the presence or absence of purpose in their lives. Since becoming interested in the importance and benefits of purpose in life, I have made a practice of interviewing people I meet who seem contented. This helps to test my hypothesis that happiness is associated with an intention to become connected to some higher purpose. Of course, I have observed many people reporting to work every day who are cynical and rusted-out, who have given up and who seem content to make it to quitting time. Many feel that while they still believe it to be morally important for them to work hard, they don't see any social or personal benefit deriving from their work; someone else just becomes richer.

However, as substantiated in Peters and Waterman's best-selling book, *In Search of Excellence*, people who perform most energetically, creatively, and enthusiastically are those who believe they are contributing to a purpose larger than themselves: in other words, when they have a **mission**. The failure of many businesses to enlist employees in some kind of unselfish, nonquantitative **mission** is at the root of many productivity problems today. When we ignore purpose values at work we inhibit the highest motivator.

Having a clear sense of purpose—one that goes beyond oneself—has many productive consequences. It provides us with a source of enthusiasm and energy and a goal to strive for. We are clear as to how others may benefit from our efforts. Purpose orders our life experiences and provides principles for our conduct. Purpose gives meaning to our lives and, perhaps most importantly, makes us feel good—alive! In my interviews I have found among many people a strong desire to "make a life, not just a living."

A missing piece in job satisfaction and productivity is a process for helping people find a sense of purpose or direction for their talents, a process which helps people:

- to identify their most motivating talents.
- to use their talents to further some issue or interest they care about.
- to locate or create work environments that fit "who they are" (their values and life-style preferences).
- to learn how to "pay the price" (i.e., understand risk-taking as an essential step toward getting what they want).

The notion of discovering or choosing the work you do may take a while to digest. A high degree of motivation is usually needed to dream a work dream worth dreaming! It requires risk-taking, and—above all—patience. The discovery of your purpose often requires an incubation period. The architect, LeCorbusier, said that the birth of a project was just like the birth of a child: **"There's a long period of gestation . . . a lot of work in the subconscious before I make the first sketch. That lasts for months. One fine morning the project has taken form without my knowing it."**

Several additional processes are also important to discovering your purpose and acting on it:

- *Risk-taking*. Each life decision is a point at which we face the challenge of how we will use our potential.

All life is a risk; each decision point has its own uncertainties.

Fortune favors the bold! Have your skills ready to capitalize on an opportunity. Most opportunities don't come labeled "big break." Take off the blinders about the way things **should** happen. Don't fall into the justice trap. Life isn't fair. Those who expect it to be often become stuck when life shortchanges them.

- *Self-Leadership*. A popular song says, "I gotta be me!" At the point of making a decision you can always follow someone's lead. Or you can check precedent. Or you can do what others expect. But in the end, it's a matter of being true to yourself. **All of us need to remind ourselves that we are working out a life that has never been lived before!** Respect hunches. Listen to your intuition and have confidence in gut feelings even if others are skeptical.

- *Strengths*. You must work hard at making decisions. But keep in mind that we tend to do best at things that use our motivated strengths. The work decision process includes failure. But life gives us second chances and in grasping them we can use our past failures creatively. We must build on our failures and focus on our strengths. Psychologist Carl Rogers put it best. **"I find I am more effective when I can listen acceptingly to myself and can be myself."** Ask yourself, "How can I fail at being myself?"

There is clearly no instant formula for discovering higher purpose and job satisfaction. Work that is centered around a clear purpose has integrity. What goes on inside us—our feelings, hopes, fears, principles, etc.—is reflected in our day-to-day work behavior. Through **working on purpose**— we have intention and integrity.

For many of us, however, an uneasiness follows a lack of purpose in our work. We sense a need to bring our daily efforts into better alignment with our values.

Earlier in our history, people offered their daily activities as a "thank you" to God (because all enterprise was ultimately intended for God). This was a basis, for the Judeo-

Christian work ethic. The concept of stewardship, by which one made an offering to God of one's best efforts, elevated a person's work to the status of purpose.

The most obvious thing about purpose from the point of view of work is that it is connected to this concept of stewardship. A theological view is that every individual is by creation essentially a steward. And this is possible because each of us has been born with and has acquired certain unique abilities. We are accountable for how they are used, misused, or not used at all. There are today many different words for describing these abilities, including: aptitudes, gifts, skills, talents, strengths, powers, etc.

In the last half-century, the concept of stewardship has diminished. At the same time, work values have changed and many work places have grown so huge and impersonal that the individual has become increasingly frustrated in his or her attempt to find meaning in work.

Most of us want to feel that we are significant and that our efforts contribute to something enduring and worthwhile. More than anything else, purpose enables people and organizations to produce results in ways consistent with their most deeply held values.

As Studs Terkel has stated in *Working*, **"Work provides us our daily bread and our daily purpose."**

Chapter 10

THE PURPOSE
INVENTORY

The question arises, how can I find purpose in the "real world?" There are no groups promoting (or opposing) purpose as a major social movement. Many people argue against the practicality of purposeful work, of ensuring the spirit of a person, or self-development and so forth. Rarely, however, does anyone argue against the idea as such.

Anyone who thinks that a determination to seek purpose is not accompanied by certain downside risks should remember this thought from Henry David Thoreau: **"If I knew ... that a man was coming to my house with the conscious design of doing me good, I should run for my life."**

"Doing good!" to others may be an expression of purest motives or it may simply be, a means of putting my talents to work on something that interests me.

The meanings and purposes in any life are many and varied. Some are detected very early; some late. Some are work-related and some are religious or social. But the power of purpose implies a relationship between a person (you, the reader) and some larger system of ideas or values. There are both commitments and rewards. We all differ as to what we are willing to commit ourselves to, and as to what will stir up our deepest motives.

For many of us there has been a sharp realization that our daily work (where, incidentally we spend forty to sixty percent of our lives) simply is not as satisfying as we want it to be.

A real question for many of us, then, is "What is going

74

to make me go to work alert and fully alive?" Most of us get up "because the alarm clock goes off," not because it makes any difference. Most of us go to work "because it's Monday," not because it makes any difference.

There appears to be a gap between supply and demand of a most central thing—**purpose-full** work—work that fully engages our skills in something we believe in.

One major reason for this gap is that many of us don't really know our skills, interests, and priorities.

Another major reason is that we don't really expect work to be fulfilling.

I have found at least four separate levels of work expectations:

1. The first level is "it's just a job; any job is okay as long as the pay is good and I can do my thing after work."
2. The second level is that of a permanent job. At this level "my work has to be regular; I need benefits, vacations, and . . . security."
3. A third level is that of profession, trade, or vocation. Rather than thinking only of money and security, "I want substance in my life. I want to use my talents and be challenged." At this level we are still profoundly concerned with income and the regard attached to the profession itself.
4. A fourth level is that of purpose-full work. "I realize that work is not related only to money, that work is a path to further learning and personal growth, and that work focuses on something I believe needs doing in this world." People begin to consider the purpose that work can serve and the opportunity it allows them to follow a personal path, yet still have a marketable, income-producing involvement in the world.

A good idea of what people expect from their work has been summarized in a study by the University of Michigan Survey Research Center. Fifteen hundred American workers representing all types of occupations were asked to rank twenty-five aspects of work. The eight elements they considered most important were:

- interesting work
- enough help and equipment to get the job done
- enough information to get the job done
- good pay
- opportunity to develop special abilities
- job security
- seeing the results of one's work

Interesting work, equitable salary, a chance to develop skills, and a sense of adequacy—the internal power to get the job done effectively—are desires that most people share. When asked about specific working conditions, a large number of respondents to the survey reported that they wanted the chance to grow on the job.

There is no formula that brings purpose to our career. It starts with reflection. We find it from the inside out. I discover that there is something unique and special that I can contribute and that the kind of work I do should relate to these special contributions.

The power of purpose is a search for work that fully engages our talents, interests, and values. This appropriate relationship with the world is what the Buddhists call "right livelihood."

Dr. Albert Schweitzer called this notion, "reverence for life." Late one afternoon in September, 1915, Dr. Schweitzer was sitting on the deck of a small steamboat making its way up the Ogooue River to Lambarene in Central Africa. He was bringing medical services to the native population in French Equatorial Africa. The boat was moving cautiously through a herd of hippopotamuses in the river. As Schweitzer watched the ship's captain maneuver to avoid hitting the animals, he came to a profound realization—the captain represented the highest purpose: reverence for the life of other creatures. For years Schweitzer had been searching for the key ethic in the modern world. He found it in Africa— "reverence for life."

Schweitzer recognized that far more people are idealistic than will admit to being so. He stated:

"Just as the water of the streams we see is small in amount compared to that which flows underground, so the idealism which becomes visible is small in amount compared with what men and women bear locked in their hearts, unreleased or scarcely released. To unbind what is bound, to bring the underground waters to the surface: mankind is waiting and longing for such as can do that."

It's an odd quirk that makes us repress our idealism. Opportunities for idealism are virtually everywhere. The key to discovering the right one for you is not to look for what should be done and simply sign up. Instead, ask "What moves me? What arouses my sense of right and wrong? What area has been neglected, where little or nothing is being done?"

Take a moment to assess some of your work purpose tendencies. **Is your work purpose-full?**

REFLECTION#14

THE PURPOSE EXAM

What are the signs in your work that indicate "Yes, my work is rich and purpose-full?" What are the signs that indicate "No, my work isn't as full and satisfying as I might wish?" Think of this inventory as you would think of taking a periodic **physical examination**. Check either yes or no according to how you feel about each question **today**.

	Yes	No
1. Do I recognize what I'm good at . . . my most enjoyed skills?	___	___
2. Do I fully utilize my most enjoyed skills in my work?	___	___

(continued)

	Yes	No
3. Does my work further some interest or issue that I care deeply about?	_____	_____
4. Do I see myself, through my work, as making a difference in the world?	_____	_____
5. Do I view most work days with a sense of enthusiasm (vs. an economic chore)?	_____	_____
6. Have I developed my own philosophy of life and success?	_____	_____
7. Am I taking the necessary risks to live my philosophy?	_____	_____
8. Do I feel a sense of meaning and purpose for my life?	_____	_____
9. Do I have written goals this year relating to my purpose?	_____	_____
10. Am I living my life now (vs. hoping that life will work out some day)?	_____	_____
Total *Yes* responses =	_____	

How To Interpret Your Score

The total *Yes* responses on The Purpose Exam provides a general idea of your quality-of-work life. Compare your total score to the Power of Purpose standards:

8-10	Excellent	You're obviously intent on making a difference through your work.
5-7	Average	You have a sense of purpose or direction, but you might consider further clarifying your commitments.

| Below 5 | Poor | You're in danger of wasting your most valuable currency—time—working at something which you don't believe makes much difference. |

Not everyone has a work purpose. Many of us haven't even thought about our purpose. Others have several purposes. Some people feel they are led to a purpose through a spiritual experience. Others are having a "crisis of purpose." Some of us have lost our purpose and are looking for a new one. Many of us fell into ours through someone else or by a strange coincidence, an unexpected event. Whatever your situation, this whole section is designed to get you thinking about work purpose because people with a work purpose are more contented and clearer about their life direction.

Here are some examples of **statements of work purposes**:

- I use my _creativity_ and leadership to _do P.R._
   (value)   (talent)

 for a _neighborhood housing group_.
     (issue)

- Because I _value family life_ and hate to
    (value)

 see _children alone at home_, I
    (issue)

 organized and now run a day care facility
     (talent)

 in our organization.

- There is _no theater_ in this town. I _use my influence_ by
   (issue)   (talent)

designing a master plan to *present to the arts council*.

It would *bring in new business and also be enjoyable*.
(value)

Of course, these purposes can be much more broadly stated as well, as long as they are carefully thought through.

I use my _____ skills to work on . . .

Public Education
Freedom of Speech and/
  or Press
Freedom of Religion
Health Care
Housing
Child Care
Family Support
Community Services
Citizen Participation in
  Politics
Job Training and
  Placement
Small Business
  Opportunities

Senior Citizen Care
Group Cultural Heritage
Peace Issues
Court System/
  Corrections
Performing Arts
Literature
Natural Resources
Architectural Quality
World Hunger

Understanding that a purpose without a solid foundation is only a daydream, we must insure that our vision is grounded in clear steps of action with measureable outcomes. We need to work systematically and focus on results.

Chapter 11

MAKING A LIVING
WORK

One of the first experiences of my professional career was a conference I attended shortly after I began my first full-time position. I was excited to meet new colleagues and have an opportunity to hear some esteemed thinkers in my field, people that I had only read of previously. Many of us new to the field listened attentively to the foremost authority deliver a rather dismal keynote address. We were told that we could look forward to increasing work loads, red tape, and a race against obsolescence. His comments were underscored by other speakers—that we must be prepared for the worst. Suddenly I had a sinking feeling about my chosen path.

I have remembered that experience on more than one occasion. Because these were extremely competent people, I was quite disturbed by the message conveyed. My problem with what was presented was that it strongly suggested that the path to work success and the ultimate achievement of work goals involved an arduous struggle.

I do agree that paying the price at some point is an essential part of achieving one's goals. My personal philosophy, however, is different. Essentially, I would argue that a satisfying career (and life) should be made as naturally enjoyable as possible. To the extent that we use our most enjoyed talents on the problem situations that hold special interest for us, we build enjoyment into our work. To the extent that we pursue worthwhile challenges that we naturally enjoy, an inner motivation is activated. The way to be effective and find happiness and meaning through our work is to discover what is needed and wanted, and then produce it—right where we are! Discovering that principle, we also discover that who we are makes a difference. We do count. The work we do does matter. We can plan our work so that we enjoyably progress toward our desired destinies. In fact, it's legitimate to enjoy what we're doing! While I believe that the speakers would agree with my rationale, the picture they portrayed, perhaps unintentionally, was one of an agonizing, uphill climb. Here's my message, which has been evolving and struggling for expression ever since that conference: **"Don't work hard to make a living; struggle to make a living work.** Pay the price but use the skills that you most naturally enjoy."

We can become successful (and enjoy a life rich in meaning) if our work is inspired. As Norman Vincent Peale said, **"Do your job naturally because you like it and success will take care of itself."**

Why bother? Good question. Personal planning does take time and offers no guarantees. Your job, however, probably takes up a number of waking hours each week. To a large degree it determines your quality of life depending on the location of the job and the kind of pay earned. Where you live, who you become friends with, and what opportunities come your way are influenced by the work you do.

When the work we do is a mismatch with what we need and enjoy in basic ways, the mental and physical costs can be high. Problems in performance can result. Advancement is not as likely, and personal frustration and stress can be wearing.

Engaging in the power of purpose process affirms that **work can be more than just a job, that it can be a means of satisfaction and contribution.** The time taken to identify elements of preferred work is well invested.

An important key to creating work enjoyment is clarifying our work values. There is a tendency to assume that we know ourselves well and do not need to enter into a reflective assessment process concerning work values.

Values play an important role in work satisfaction. We need to look at the things that we want and value in our work—things that are important to us.

Values are not right or wrong or true or false. They are personal preferences. Exploring our preferences can be somewhat difficult because we confuse what we do need with what we say we need (perhaps what is fashionable).

At certain times in our careers the need to understand our values becomes more important. We might find that we have out-grown familiar roles; certain images of ourself no longer fit. Organizational realities also have a way of forcing us to rethink our values. Career decisions are easier when we know what we value and recognize our priorities.

Work values help us to make sense of our world. Every career decision we make is based on both our work values and the economic realities of the world of work. We often select the facts on the basis of our values.

Our values are formed by our experiences with other people—family members, teachers, and groups to which we belong. All of these have a powerful effect on the formation of our work values.

On the following pages are a number of desirable factors in an ideal job.

REFLECTION #15

WORK VALUES

Look over the next few pages of values, eighteen are listed.

- Select the ten values that are the most important to you—that you want *now* (whether or not you have them).

- Number your top ten values from most important (1) to least important (10).

(continued)

- Under "comments" for each value, write in comments that truly reflect that value for you. For example, "Who do I know or see that exemplifies this value?" or "Where or what kind of job has these qualities?"

- Write in your top five most valued priorities from 1 (most important to you) to 5 (least important to you).

  1. _____
  2. _____
  3. _____
  4. _____
  5. _____

- From your most valued priorities, list those which your current work provides for and those you need more of to be fully satisfied.

My current job provides: My current job does not provide:

  1. _____   _____
  2. _____   _____
  3. _____   _____
  4. _____   _____
  5. _____   _____

Security	*Advancement*
A job which is not likely to be eliminated: assurance of career longevity and a reasonable financial reward.	A job that provides opportunity to grow, move up the ladder, be able to get ahead rapidly; aspiring.
Comments:	Comments:

Contribution Opportunity to have a direct impact on the success of the enterprise, making a lasting contribution or legacy. Comments:	*Money/Status* Purchase essentials and luxuries; prosperous life-style; gain respect of friends, family, and community. High earnings anticipated; title. Comments:
Independence Make decisions about one's work; manage oneself; opportunity to work independently according to my time schedule; self reliant; do projects by myself. Comments:	*Purpose* A job that makes a difference; creates value; service resulting in benefits to others; feel that my work is contributing to needs I feel are very important. Comments:
Recognition/Expertise Self and work known and approved by others; desire to be known/famous; job that is viewed as important in the enterprise; well regarded in one's field; public credit for work well done. Comments:	*Environment* Pleasant working conditions; work place that is well designed; dress appropriate to my self-image. Comments:
Variety New and different challenges; opportunity for much new growth and learning; frequent changes in content and setting. Comments:	*Balance* Job that leaves time for pursuits outside of work (e.g., family, personal, leisure, community); duties that follow a largely predictable schedule; weekends, evenings, vacation times available. Comments:

(continued)

Challenge/Competition Personal/professional feelings of accomplishment; problem-solving as core part of job; work in time-pressured circumstances; role that pits my abilities against others; high-paced activity. Comments:	*Entrepreneurship* Motivation to be self-determining; motivation to develop a new product or service; desire to define oneself through one's work; personal control through ownership. Comments:
Location Geographic location conducive to life-style; community where I can become involved; relocation options. Comments:	*Relationships* Belonging; working with a team; frequent and open interpersonal contact with others; develop close personal relationships as a result of work activity; friendly, compatible people. Comments:
Adventure/Risk Situations with risk and flair; job that stretches my resources and abilities to meet new situations; being on the "cutting edge." Comments:	*Comfort* Low pressure; few constraints; job that is fairly systematized and unchanging; opportunity to let others set expectations and direction; contentedness; enjoyable; leisurely life; avoid rat race in job role. Comments:

Leadership	Creativity
Responsibility for directing the work of others; to be held accountable for important tasks; authority and power to decide courses of action, policies, etc.; influence people and/or events. Comments:	Solving new problems and tasks according to one's own standards; opportunity to innovate and create new ideas, programs, products, etc.; chance to create and contribute to something successful or beautiful or clever. Comments:

REFLECTION #16

WORK VALUES DIALOGUE

One of the simplest ways to sort out your work values is by the manner in which you express them verbally. We all tend to articulate our values in characteristic ways. For example, people who say of their work, "It's a living," are revealing a lot more about their values than they may think they are. Once the focus of your work values is identified, it becomes much easier to pay attention to your sense of purpose.

The subject of work values triggers many feelings and crystalizes many thoughts. Complete the following unfinished sentences. Allow approximately twenty minutes to complete the exercise. You should not think too long or labor too much over the construction of your answers.

After listing your principal concerns about your work:
- Read your answers out loud.
- Read your answers to a spouse, friend, or trusted colleague. Use "I" statements; such as "I believe . . . ," "I feel . . . ," "I am . . . ." Be as honest with yourself and your partner in dialogue as you can be.

1. A paycheck is _____
_____

(continued)

2. My feeling about the purpose and use of money is _____
_____

3. Most people I know feel that their jobs _____
_____

4. Job satisfaction for me means _____
_____

5. The hardest part of defining my work values is __
_____

6. The worst job I ever had was _____
_____

7. What made it so bad was _____
_____

8. The best job I ever had was _____
_____

9. What made it so good was _____
_____

10. I've been told that I'd be good at _____
_____

11. My wildest career dream is to someday _____
_____

12. I believe it is or is not important for me to establish a sense of purpose at this time _____
_____

Chapter 12

MYTHS ABOUT PURPOSE

The following are four commonly held, erroneous beliefs that can be obstacles to our moving ahead toward a purpose. As you read each one, ask yourself, "Do I believe this?"

Myth 1: To have purpose means to do something completely new.

Can you think of anything that is totally new? Every idea or thing created is an extension or synthesis of previous ideas. New scientific breakthroughs are built on existing fundamental truths. Most new ideas are the result of reorganizing and applying the ideas of others. Like runners in a relay race, we simply carry the baton another leg of the race. As you see a purpose, accept the fact that at the heart of most new ideas is the borrowing, adding, combining, or modifying of old ones.

Myth 2: Only a special minority of people have purpose in their lives.

This is the most commonly rationalized of all myths. There is no denying that often we have relied on experts to solve many of our problems. History, however, is filled with great innovations made by people with virtually no expertise in the areas where they made their mark. Being a novice is often an asset because we aren't hemmed in by traditional ways of viewing a situation.

Purpose appears in proportion to the energies we expend, rather than to any degree of expertness.

It's the drive to make a difference that seems to count most.

Myth 3: Purpose is like magic; you either have it or you don't.

The "pop-in" theory of motivation would have you believe that creative ideas or new directions are flashes of brilliance that suddenly appear to a fortunate few. Purpose descends on the lucky recipient. If you believe that—nothing will happen for sure! Meaning comes to those who work for it. Any successful person can attest to the absurdity of "waiting" to be inspired. First you begin. Then the insights appear. As psychologist Albert Ellis states,

> **"The best years of your life are the ones in which you decide your problems are your own. You don't blame them on your mother, the ecology or the President. You realize that you control your own destiny."**

The paradox of purpose is that in order to address new solutions to problems we must first familiarize ourselves with the ideas of others. The ideas form a base for launching our own purposes. Gather as much information as you can (realizing that you'll never have enough). Make a decision. Get on with the business of living and working on purpose.

Myth 4: Purpose is nice, but impractical.

Many times we become so rutted in day-to-day survival activity that we lose sight of what we're doing and our activity becomes a false end in itself rather than a means to an end. Thoreau put it bluntly. **"It isn't enough to be busy. Ants are busy."**

The question we should ask ourselves is: "What are we busy about?"

"Gee, I'd love to get involved, but who's got the time?

I have a spouse, job, children, and social commitments. How on earth can you expect me to find the time?" Sound familiar? For most of us time is indeed the scarce resource. Few of us have enough, but everyone has all there is!

Waiting until you have the time is as futile as trying to save money by putting away what you don't happen to spend. Busyness is often a blanket that hides fear. By keeping busy we avoid having to face the possibility of failure. The only way to commit time to a purpose is to "steal it" from some other present activity. This is what the power of purpose is all about.

Every new idea evokes three stages of reaction:

1. "It's impossible (or crazy). Don't waste your time."
2. "It's possible, but why do it? It's just not worth it."
3. "I said it was a good idea all along."

The critics of the world gravitate toward new ideas, and critics are everywhere. It's much easier to criticize than to risk and that's why they're everywhere. Criticism soothes their conscience by giving them a false sense of superiority.

You can plan for your work and life just as accurately and easily as you plan your vacation or any other worthwhile endeavor. You are the judge as to how complex or simple your plan should be—this will depend on your preferred way of thinking.

Everybody looks for excuses. It's natural to try to blame someone or something else for our dilemmas. A few of the most popularly used excuses include:

- "I'm too young."
- "I don't have the right experience."
- "There are no jobs."
- "I don't know what I want to do."
- "My field is not hiring."
- "I may have to give up something I like."
- "My hours may be longer."
- "My performance may depend on the performance of others."

- "I may have to act as a change agent."
- "The direction may not be as clear as for my present assignments."
- "I may have to spend more time planning."
- "My mistakes may be more visible."
- "The pressure may be greater."
- "My actions and decisions may come under heavy criticism."
- "I may have to cooperate with people I dislike."

All things considered, choosing a **purpose-full** job or career is a major decision. It will be, of course, a decision made several times in the course of a lifetime, sometimes under pressure to get a paycheck fast; at other times, a more relaxed and gradual process. However the circumstances may vary, the impact of the jobs we take is great.

You are likely to make a dozen major work decisions in your lifetime. It is in your best interest to make those decisions with as much information as possible.

Increasing shifts in the economy and the work world emphasize the growing importance for you to do more on your own in shaping your career instead of relying on others for direction and control.

Change in some form is inevitable. A key consideration in living a satisfying life is what you do about influencing the nature and outcome of change. Change takes time. Most changes require a series of events to occur in some evolving way. You can help some or all of these events to occur. Choice, not chance, can determine your work life.

REFLECTION #17

LIVING AND WORKING—ON PURPOSE

Review the following life-style and work-style questions, and check those that most closely reflect your life, work, or special situation. The list contains many questions but is by no means all-inclusive.

#17A

WHEN THERE ARE QUESTIONS ABOUT LIVING—ON PURPOSE	. . . CONSISTENTLY EXPRESSED IN TERMS LIKE THESE
1. What type of work fits with my lifestyle?	_____ "I'd be happier in my job if I felt I really fit in."
2. Where do I want to live?	_____ "Relocation would be hard on my teenagers."
3. What do I want out of life?	_____ "I have a feeling that life is going by and I'm not getting what I want out of it."
4. What trade-offs should I make in order to reach my career goals?	_____ "There's no point in trying to do any planning. How can I outguess what the future will bring?"
5. Which factors do I and don't I control in pursuing my career goals?	_____ "I feel like I don't have any control over what's happening to me."
6. How can I fit together parenting and my work life?	_____ "With both of us pursuing careers and the kids in school, I couldn't even think of making a move at the present time."

(continued)

. . . And if you have agreed with three or more of these statements, then the focus of your concern is **life planning** and some resources to investigate are:

The Inventurers: Excursions in Life and Career Renewal by Janet Hagberg and Richard Leider

If You Don't Know Where You're Going, You'll Probably End Up Somewhere Else by David Campbell

The Three Boxes of Life by Richard N. Bolles

Pathfinders by Gail Sheehy

Self-Renewal by John Gardner

Taking Stock: A Daily Self-Management Journal by Richard Leider & James Harding

#17B

WHEN THERE ARE QUESTIONS ABOUT WORKING—ON PURPOSE	. . . CONSISTENTLY EXPRESSED IN TERMS LIKE THESE
7. What tasks and relationships would I find most rewarding?	_____ "What I want and what the company wants may not be the same thing."
8. What career paths are realistic and achievable for me?	_____ "When you get to be my age, you're pretty much locked into one path."
9. How do I get out of a boring situation?	_____ "This is a dead-end job. There's nowhere for someone like me to go from here."
10. What are the kinds of special training and experience I need to advance in my chosen career?	_____ "Career planning sounds nice. But you know and I know it just isn't possible."

| 11. How can I stretch my capabilities to their limits within my present job? | _____ "The boss would have a fit if I even mentioned making a change." |
| 12. Who should I talk with about career decisions? | _____ "Things have been going pretty well for me. I'd better let well enough alone." |

. . . and if you have agreed with three or more of these statements, then the focus of your concerns is **career planning** and some resources to investigate are:

What Color is Your Parachute?
by Richard N. Bolles

Career Strategies
by Andrew H. Souerwine

The Complete Job Search Handbook
by Howard Figler

The Truth About You
by Arthur Miller and Ralph T. Mattson

Career Satisfaction and Success
by Bernard Haldane

#17C
WHEN THERE ARE QUESTIONS ABOUT SPECIAL SITUATIONS

. . . CONSISTENTLY EXPRESSED IN TERMS LIKE THESE

| 13. How can I be more assertive? | _____ "I'm shy, let's face it. Getting ahead here is going to be different for me." |
| 14. How can I establish more effective relationships? | _____ "I live for my work. I wouldn't know what to do with myself if I didn't have this job to go to." |

(continued)

15. How can I determine some new leisure interests?

_____ "My life balance is out of whack."

16. What educational options are open to me?

_____ "The only way I can change the career track is by going back to school. But how do I manage that at my age?"

17. How can I plan for my retirement?

_____ "I might just as well serve out my time. I'm too close to retirement to do anything else."

18. How can I manage stress in my career/life?

_____ "Something's got to give. I'm not sure I can handle the increased responsibility at work and a family too."

. . . and if you have agreed with three or more of these statements, then the focus of your concerns is on **special situation planning** and some resources to investigate are:

Wellness Workbook: A Guide to Attaining High Level Wellness
by Regina Sara Ryan and John W. Travis

Hope for the Flowers
by Trina Paulus

Shyness: What It Is, What to Do About It
by Philip Zimbardo

So You Want to Go Back to School?
by Elinor Lenz and Marjorie Hansen

I Need to Have You Know Me
by Roland and Doris Larson

Section IV

TAPPING THE POWER OF PURPOSE

Chapter 13

THE SOURCES OF PURPOSE

Where do you start? How do you decide where to commit yourself? Where have you chosen already to commit yourself and your resources (time and money)? What small steps have you taken already? It's a question of personal choice. We have only a certain amount of personal resources—time, energy, and finances.

William Least Heat Moon, in his *Blue Highways*, explored some of these issues as he traveled the back roads (the ones marked in blue by Rand McNally) of America. Near Hat Creek, California, he met an old fellow traveling with a dog and a German woman. Having left behind his job, the old man said reflectively:

> **"A man's never out of work if he's worth a damn. It's just sometimes he doesn't get paid. I've gone unpaid my share and I've pulled my share of pay. But that's got nothing to do with working. A man's work is doing what he's supposed to do, and that's why he needs a catastrophe now and again to show him a bad turn isn't the end, because a bad stroke never stops a good man's work."**

There's an important distinction here between one's **work** and one's **job**.

Another of Moon's characters says, "A job's what you force yourself to pay attention to for money. With work, you don't have to force yourself."

Work is paying attention to what matters most—to making a difference in life. Yet it's never enough to just complain about our job, and, perhaps, hit the open road in search of "work."

What about you? What's your work these days?

Your work is the principles you live by transformed into action. Open your eyes to the world around you and notice the endless work that calls for your response.

Read the paper.

Watch TV specials.

Study your organization's long-range plans.

Go to speeches and demonstrations.

Talk to others about their commitments.

Subscribe to newsletters.

Find out where your church is investing its efforts.

Read your political party's platform.

For most of us the world in which we live is rich with possibilities for gaining greater meaning and direction. To tap the power of purpose, we need to see the potential work that is all around us.

Viktor Frankl points to three ways to discover purpose: ". . . we can discover this meaning in life in three different ways: 1. by doing a deed; 2. by experiencing a value; and 3. by suffering."

1. *"Doing a Deed"*   One way to start is to "discover" what's needed and wanted, and then produce it—right where you are—in your current work, family, church, or community.

Visible achievement and accomplishment of deeds—especially those we have had something to say about creating—are important. These can seem trivial to an outsider but they are important from a personal perspective. For deeds to have a real impact at a personal level, we must own the objective in a personally committed way. Claiming some deed set by others or expected of us is not nearly as satisfying or purpose-full. This, however, does not mean that whatever deed or objectives we select need to be large or even visible to others. It is the "do-gooders," as we discussed earlier, who need to keep score of their virtues. "Keeping score" may actually reduce our sense of contentment as we clearly see how our commitment is driven by external (or ego) influences.

2. *"Experiencing a Value"* Our core of values and principles guide much of our behavior. If identified and clear to us, a superordinate value can serve as a source of purpose (if we are able to consistently live it!). The reverse is also true. When circumstances or our own weaknesses lead us to act counter to our core values, we feel poorly about ourselves and we can become depressed and angry.

For example, I truly value strong family relationships. If I need to travel too often or work especially long hours at my job, I feel torn. My behavior is inconsistent with my values and I feel guilty and depressed. I feel the conflict between my deeply held value and my behavior. Yet, I do have a clear choice. I can take action to behave in ways consistent with my values. I have, for example, made a deliberate choice to maintain my travel schedule at a maximum of five days a month or sixty days per year. Some months I do travel more. But, I take summers off for writing, reflection, and family time. I feel the integrity and "the power" that come from "walking my talk"—behaving consistently with my deepest held values and principles.

3. *"Suffering"* There are specific kinds of crises that significantly reduce the quality of life for most of us. These events are so devastating that our entire sense of meaning may slip, leaving us shaken or enraged. At such times, feelings of shock and being in limbo are not uncommon. When we cope effectively, a purpose may actually be found or strengthened or made clearer. We often learn more about who we really are under conditions of "suffering". The following are examples of "triggering events;" they are listed in order of the impact that they seem to have on most of us:

- Death of spouse
- Divorce
- Marital separation
- Jail term
- Death of a close family member
- Personal illness
- Discharge from work
- Retirement
- Financial reversals

These kinds of events, at least temporarily, cause most of us to wonder whether we really have worth, whether we are acceptable as persons. Our self-esteem, and the basic sense of who we are, often are torn apart and we are cut off from the purpose and meaning we need so much.

We begin to ask ourselves the "Who am I?" and "What if—?" questions and to consider the possibility of new roles and relationships. In the early stages, the process is one of a grasping search for new sources of self-esteem to fill the blank spaces produced by the loss. But with time, the pain subsides and gradually gives way to some hope about the future—some new images of ourselves. Our time becomes occupied with growing in new ways. As we adapt to the change and normalize our lives, we feel empowered with new confidence and competence. And, for some of us, the personal sense of who we really are, our purpose, will change markedly.

Chapter 14

THE POWER WITHOUT THE PURPOSE

What kinds of skills, abilities, and strengths do I have? What type of environment could I best live and work in? How can I best utilize my talents for something in which I believe (a value, product, service, ideal, problem, organization, etc.)?

One of the major elements in this **purpose process** is clarifying your skills—those which you already have and are motivated to use and those which you would like to develop.

Although skills are a part of everyday vocabulary, few people can state clearly what their "**most enjoyed**" skills are. The power behind your purpose is your skills—particularly those you are most motivated to develop and use. In this chapter you are asked to complete a simple Strengths Inventory—a short list of your enjoyed skills. Working with the Inventory should help you begin the process of empowering your purpose.

You have every reason to enter this stage of the process with great optimism because you already possess many skills and valuable personal traits. This fundamental assumption has proved true for everyone who has used this process. Each of us possesses hundreds of skills and valuable personal traits (and at least a few talents). Many of us might deny that this is the case simply because we have never looked for our strengths, systematically, and are therefore unaware of them.

Talents ... Who Me?

You may perform a skill so effortlessly and superbly that you often forget you have it. This is a "talent." You might not have had to pay the price to learn this skill because it came so easily or you were born with it. You may never have had to practice it extensively.

The Puritan ethic has convinced many of us that "anything requiring hard work is valuable and anything that comes easily and does not require hard work is worth-less." About our talents we often think, "This comes easily, so it must be worth-less."

Actually, your talents are your most powerful skills of all.

If you're confused as to what your strengths are, ask your spouse, a friend, a co-worker, supervisor, or someone who knows you very well to help you to clarify and reinforce your strengths.

You can expand and sharpen your awareness of your strengths by asking three people whom you respect, to listen as you describe skills you feel you are good at. They will help you see more skills and talents. (*Important*: Don't get hung-up on modesty!)

If you wish to spend the time and energy to discover or confirm your skills in some depth, you might consider reading one of these resource books with good skills sections:

- *The Inventurers* by Janet Hagberg and Richard Leider
- *The Truth About You* by Arthur Miller and Ralph Mattson
- *Career Satisfaction and Success* by Bernard Haldane
- *What Color Is Your Parachute?* by Richard Bolles

These and other resources will help you take a deeper look at your skills than is intended in this book.

"Most Enjoyed" Skills?

The idea that you should enjoy your work is one you may both accept and question. **Yet it seems to make sense that we do best at that which we enjoy most.** There's always the idea that work is something to be tolerated and play is something to be enjoyed. What's your attitude toward work? Also, work consumes a significant number of your waking hours. When you consider both of those ideas, it might seem to be good common sense to clarify and use your most enjoyed skills.

A skill is something you can do and do well.

In contrast to a few obvious skills that might emerge early in life (art, music, math, etc.), we detect most of our skills more slowly and they are more difficult to recognize when they appear.

Everyone learns to feel that some skills are more valuable to society than others. Thus, many of us don't acknowledge some of our talents because we believe, "I'm really not that good at it" or "What good could that talent possibly be?"

Many of us also have a limited vocabulary when we try to describe our strengths. Thus, a vocabulary must be created in order for us to name our skills.

Knowing yourself—what you do well and like doing, what motivates you, what you value, and how you see your life and work—is important not only for making career decisions but also for empowering a purpose. Any work decision should be based on your answer to the question, "Is this work likely to be a good match for my strongest skills or one in which I'll be able to grow and develop?"

Your skills have probably been demonstrated in experiences which you feel have represented achievements.

By identifying and studying your achievements you will find an underlying pattern of skills you have repeatedly used to make these achievements happen.

An effective way to elicit your skills from past experiences is to write short sketches about them.

As you develop a list of achievements, it is important that you:

- Decide what is a meaningful achievement for you. (Never mind what other people say.)
- Acknowledge that all your achievements, no matter where or when you performed them, involve skills.

105

(You will be surprised to discover how many skills you can identify in even minor achievements.)
- Consider for each achievement:
    —Was it meaningful to me then or now that I did it?
    —Did I have a great desire to do it at the time?
    —Would I do it over again if I had the chance?

REFLECTION #18

For this exercise you will need seven 3" × 5" cards.

On each of the seven cards, list a past achievement you feel good about. List experiences in which you felt a sense of real satisfaction or enjoyment. Include big things and little things. Each day there is something you do that feels more satisfying or closer to being an achievement than others (e.g., projects, speeches, reports, chairing a meeting, solving a problem). Don't look for dramatic or unusual examples.

Then on the back of each of your seven cards, write a paragraph describing the experience. What did you "do" to accomplish what you did?

Now sort the seven cards in order from most to least important.

On each of the seven paragraphs, circle the *one word* that best describes what made the experience meaningful to you.

Write a statement about yourself *using each of the seven words* you circled. Do this any way you like; using complete sentences is not important and it need not make sense to anyone but yourself!

Example: "My achievements seemed to point out that I'm good at *trouble-shooting* problems, *organizing* meetings, *brainstorming* solutions, *summarizing* ideas, and *writing* reports."

Now write below the 5 "most enjoyed" skills (significant words) that stood out for you in your achievements.

1. _____
2. _____
3. _____
4. _____
5. _____

What does this information mean?

Knowing your "most enjoyed" skills can help you choose the options in life and work which effectively utilize your strengths.

If you find that your most enjoyed skills lie outside work positions available to you, you need to consider whether to continue to work in the organization and find outside meaningful options for your skills (i.e., community, church, club) or to find ways that your skills might fit a new type of work situation.

REFLECTION #19

STRENGTHS INVENTORY

To help you further clarify your strengths, this exercise serves as a reminder and will indicate if your skills are more general or oriented toward a specific area such as **data**, **people, or things**.

Scan the Strengths Inventory to become familiar with it. Under the column labeled "I'm good at" put a check next to the skills you have. You don't have to be an expert at the skill but you have to enjoy doing it. What you want to find out from the list is what you enjoy doing.

For those you have checked, give evidence of how and where you have used those skills and what specific results you had.

Indicating what you're good at (for example, *writing*) does not convey a complete thought. When you use these

(continued)

skills words, complete the thought by adding a phrase that describes how, where, with what or whom you used this skill.

Skills are performed on a thing, a person, or some data. (Examples: "I'm good at writing . . . minutes, memos, and surveys." "I'm good at analyzing . . . budgets.")

Now, mark each of the "I'm good at" skills with one of the following four letters indicating the degree of your proficiency in performing or applying each skill to specific situations:

A—Very competent
B—Reasonably competent
C—Developing competence
D—Wish to develop competence

List your "A's" below:
1. _____
2. _____
3. _____
4. _____

_____

"I'm good at . . ."   **My Strengths:**

_____   _____
_____   _____
_____   _____
_____   _____
_____   _____
_____   _____
_____   _____
_____   _____
_____   _____
_____   _____
_____   _____
_____   _____
_____   _____

Group A: Skills with Data

Analyzing/Evaluating
Planning/Maneuvering
Computing/Calculating
Compiling, Pulling Together
Abstract Reasoning
Coordinating Information
Synthesizing, Combining Facts
  or Ideas
Identifying Essential Point or
  Problem
Writing/Conceiving
Other

Group B: People Skills

Administering/Maintaining
Coordinating People's Work/
  Motivating
Coaching/Listening
Interviewing/Investigating
Overseeing/Supervising

Controlling/Scheduling
Teaching/Advising/Consulting
Persuading, Convincing, Selling
Assisting/Acting as Liaison
Handling Conflict, Smoothing
  Disagreements
Other

Group C: Skills with Things

Assembling/Making
Designing/Drawing
Organizing Space
Organizing Mechanical
  Operations
Fixing, Keeping In Order
Precision Handling
Operating Mechanical Things
Clerical Skills
Inventing, Developing, Setting
  Up
Other

Evidence:
How, Where,
With What or Whom
You Use This Skill

My Competency Level

_____

_____

_____

_____

_____

_____

_____

_____

_____

_____

_____

_____

_____

Chapter 15

THE PURPOSE
WITHOUT THE POWER

Now that you have identified what you're good at—the power—where do you apply your skills—to what purpose? An important next step is to clarify your areas of interest. Discover what moves you. This is the hardest part for many of us. There's an old adage: "Anything worth doing is worth doing well." Most of the emphasis has been put on the "worth doing well." This chapter, however, deals with "what's worth doing?"—a much neglected area for many of us.

When you have a good idea of what are your motivated skills (the power), and what moves you (the purpose), you have **the power of purpose.** Life and work decisions based on the power of purpose are likely to be satisfying and produce a feeling of "aliveness" in you.

"Someone Really Oughta. . . ."

To consider potential opportunities where you can make a difference and simultaneously fulfill your personal needs and wants, this exercise asks you to "discover what is needed and wanted," to think of needs in your work organization, your family, your community, or society in general, and to examine those problems, issues, or concerns that you truly feel "someone really oughta" do something about. What are the needs of people, of your family, neighborhood, community, business, church, the world? What needs doing? What actions would give you and others a better chance, a better quality of life?

REFLECTION #20

MY INTERESTS

To stimulate your thinking, use these questions or the Purpose Catalog in the next chapter.

1. What kinds of TV specials do you tend to watch? If you were asked to create a TV special, what would it be about?
2. What magazines intrigue you most at a newsstand?
3. If you started a small business in order to solve a problem, what would it be?
4. What issue would you like to see someone write a clear and concise book about?
5. What subjects would you like to learn about? Go back to school for?
6. In the past two years, what were your four favorite books? What interests do they reflect?
7. Who are the people you find yourself voluntarily getting together with, again and again? What are their interests or commitments?
8. How would you use a gift of a million dollars if it had to be designated for **purposeful** activities?
9. Is there anything you believe in so strongly you'd work at it full-time if you were paid to do it?

In the following exercise, list in the left-hand column as many things as you can that you really believe "need doing" or are "needed and wanted." Try to list at least ten. Then for each issue indicate whether **you** would be willing to commit yourself in some way to this particular need or issue.

If your answer is **yes** (even an unsure yes) to personal commitment, then use the third column to brainstorm. Describe some ways you might commit your strengths. Focus on what strengths (power) you could bring to the need or issue. List who or where you could get further information about the need, problem or issue. Jot down the names of resource people or sounding boards that might have insight and information in your areas of interest.

EXAMPLE A				"SOMEBODY REALLY OUGHTA..."	
"Oughta Be Done By Someone..."	Personal Commitment			Actions I Might Take...	Who Can Provide Further Info?
	?	Yes	No		
End Hunger and Starvation				Attend a "Hunger Project" Briefing	The Hunger Project
				Host a "Hunger Project" Briefing	World Health Organization
				Communicate the facts to the following people...	Save the Children Organization
				Write a letter to the editor	United Way
				Communicate to my Congressperson	U.N.I.C.E.F.
				Research local food-shelves program	Local churches or synagogues
				Fast one day a month (give money saved to hunger cause)	

"SOMEBODY REALLY OUGHTA . . ."

EXAMPLE B

"Oughta Be Done By Someone . . ."	Personal Commitment ?	Yes	No	Actions I Might Take . . .	Who Can Provide Further Info?
Curing Cancer				Counsel at a clinic	*The Power of Purpose* (movie)
				Work in hospice	American Cancer Society
				Investigate training programs	Janet Williams (neighbor)
				Assist in health screenings	University of Minnesota—Continuing Education
				Assist in fundraising/ membership drives/ open my own wallet	Phil Adams (Hospice Administrator)
				Research the issue	St. Luke's Church Committee
				Write articles	Yellow pages of the phone book
				Visit homes regularly	
				Develop a preventive program at local school	
				Develop a lecture series	
				Assist with in-service training for employees	
				Provide a listening ear for cancer patients	

"SOMEBODY REALLY OUGHTA..."

EXAMPLE C	"Oughta Be Done By Someone..."	Personal Commitment			"Actions I Might Take..."	Who Can Provide Further Info?
		?	Yes	No		
	Create a dialogue between nurses and nursing administration (following nurses' strike)				Discussions with union reps. (other industries)	State Nurses Association
					Scan literature	State Board of Nursing
					Create a "Dialogue" group in hospital	City Community College
					Write column in newsletter	Barbara Carter (Director of Nurses)
					Lead informational forums	Articles and workshops on "Future of Nursing" and "Conflict Management"
					Study hospital mission statement (goals of nursing division)	

"SOMEBODY REALLY OUGHTA . . ."					
	"Oughta Be Done By Someone . . ."	Personal Commitment		Actions I Might Take . . .	Who Can Provide Further Info?
		?	Yes	No	

Chapter 16

THE PURPOSE CATALOG

If you're still looking for an interest or issue, try one of those suggested in the Purpose Catalog on the following pages.

You can gradually develop a sense of purpose by gathering further information about your interests. To live is to grow; and to grow is to live. The great English biologist, Sir Julian Huxley, who spent his lifetime studying life and growth, said: "Having to decide what we will do with our leisure is inevitably forcing us to re-examine the purpose of human existence and to ask what fulfillment really means."

While we certainly want to engage in some of our interests just for sheer enjoyment and leisure, the kinds of interests most conducive to growth and fulfillment are likely to be those that (1) challenge and utilize your strengths, (2) move you!

It is important to have a perspective from which to approach questions about your chosen commitments, and a way to determine if you can make a difference through your participation.

What questions should I ask?

Many people considering purposeful commitments ask themselves these questions:

- How will I be viewed by the community in which I choose to commit myself?
- Are **they** open to new approaches to solving problems, utilizing skills, etc.?

- What is the history of this issue, organization, etc.?
- What have been some of the obstacles to success in the past?
- What changes (if any) will this commitment make in my life-style?
- What's in this for me? (Be honest in considering your career aspirations and interests as well as your altruistic considerations.)
- Can I "taste it first?" (Trial participation is often the best way to decide.)

REFLECTION #21

PAST PURPOSE

Purposes or issues to which I have committed myself in the past three years:

1. _____
2. _____
3. _____
4. _____
5. _____

Select one. On a scale of 1 to 5, circle the degree to which the following statements describe your feelings:

My role in_____

(Organization)

was_____

(Role)

I feel . . .

	Low				High
1. My skills were valuable to this organization.	1	2	3	4	5
2. The service I performed was interesting.	1	2	3	4	5
3. My time was well spent.	1	2	3	4	5

(continued)

117

I feel . . .

	Low				High
4. I received enough information to be effective.	1	2	3	4	5
5. I felt a sense of purpose in the organization's mission.	1	2	3	4	5
6. I was liked and respected by others.	1	2	3	4	5
7. There was an opportunity to develop new skills and talents.	1	2	3	4	5
8. I received adequate recognition and rewards for my efforts.	1	2	3	4	5
9. My family supported and encouraged my involvement.	1	2	3	4	5
10. This organization added to the community's quality of life.	1	2	3	4	5
	1	2	3	4	5
Total Score =					

If you scored 40 to 50, the experience could be classified as "highly satisfying." If you scored 25 to 40, the experience might have provided "average satisfaction." If you scored 25 and below, the experience might be deemed "not satisfying."

The Purpose Catalog

Let's be businesslike about this and run through a Catalog of possible new interests for you to try-on. Review the Catalog. Are there any areas that move you to act—today?

AGED/HANDICAPPED

Blind and Visually Handicapped

Veterans

Deaf and Hearing-Impaired

Fixed Incomes

Developmentally Disabled

Barrier-Free Access

Special Olympics

Hotlines Facilities

Speech Disorders

Aging Populations

Meaningful Leisure

Medical Assistance

Legal and Welfare Advocacy and Referral

Homebound Services

Housing Standards

Crime Protection

Group Homes/ Residential

HEALTH CARE

Hospices/Health Care Facilities

Smoking, Alcohol, Drug Education

First Aid and Safety

Chemical Dependency

Wellness

Emergency Food and Clothing

Nutrition and Malnutrition

Medical and Dental Research

Disease (Cancer, Heart, Blood, etc.)

COMMUNITY SERVICE

Kinship Programs (Big Brothers and Sisters, etc.)

Problems of the Poor

Disaster Relief

Educational Quality/ Literacy

Voter Registration

Civil Rights; Justice

Economic, Social, Political Oppression

Political Change

Prison Reform

(continued)

119

COMMUNITY SERVICE (CONTINUED)

Animal Services

Housing/Neighborhood Improvement

Consumer Information/ Complaints

Citizen Advocacy

Crime and Delinquency

Emergency Services

Charitable Groups

Hot Lines

The Arts/Culture

Nonviolence; Pacifism

Nuclear Movement

Human Rights

Legal Rights; Freedom

International Education/ Cross-cultural Experiences

Education on Abortion; Right to Life

Mental Health/ Retardation

Refugee Resettlement

World Hunger

Migrant Worker Conditions

Apartheid

WOMEN/MEN CHILDREN/FAMILY

Homemaker Services

Family Planning

Day Care

Special Education

Employment of Youth

Crisis Shelter; Temporary Foster Care

Money Management

Abuse (Physical, Sexual)

Education of the Gifted

Adoption

Education of Parents

Single Parenting

Men's Organizations

Women's Organizations

SPIRITUALITY

Religious Service Organizations

Mission Work

Family-life Education

Youth Outreach

Religious Education

Crisis Intervention

Emergency Social Service

SPIRITUALITY (CONTINUED)

Ecumenical Movement

Social-Action Groups

WORK

Employment (Older Worker, Youth, etc.)

Productivity

Human Relations

Minority Businesses

ENVIRONMENT

Energy Alternatives

Fuel Sources

Pollution (Air, Water, Acid Rain)

Urban Life-styles/ Renewal

Weatherization

Recycling

Agriculture

Recreation (National Parks, Wild Rivers)

Preservation of Nature

Mass Transit

Litter

Endangered Species

Population

Nuclear Waste

Volunteerism

Worker Safety

Quality of Work Life

Migrant Workers

Unemployment; Underemployment

Financial Counseling

Equal Employment Opportunities

Obsolescence

Future of Work

Retirement

LIVING AT RISK

Chapter 17

RISKING TO MAKE A DIFFERENCE

"When people are free to do as they please, they usually imitate each other."

—Eric Hoffer

What do you really want in your life? Which of your interests are really important to you?

Ideas or interests that violate or change accepted norms of behavior will likely bounce you against the barriers of conformity. We are a "norming" society. A social mirror is constantly before us (e.g., via television, magazines, advertisements, etc.) to remind us of the norms that they set for our happiness and fulfillment. The easy way out is to be "norm-al"; forget your vision and be like everyone else.

People, however, respect the risk-takers of the world! The critics are often thinking . . .

"Why didn't I think of that?"

"I wish I were that talented."

"I wish I could take a risk like that!"

"I wish my life had aliveness like that."

There will always be plenty of critics. As Albert Einstein said, "Great spirits have always encountered violent opposition from mediocre minds."

People like Socrates, Gandhi, Churchill, and Jesus were scorned in their own times for their crazy individualism and then defied later on when it was safe to do so. Why is it that every society seems to honor its live conformists and its dead troublemakers?

125

Why do people leave the comfort and security of their daily routines to engage in risks that subject them to stress and loss? What possible value do they derive from living at risk?

Obviously people engage in these things in order to experience something which they cannot experience in their daily routines. One cannot enjoy the mountain view without the risk of the climb, so the risk is taken. In a risk situation, away from routine, emotions surge up and are released. Many people may not realize they are engulfed in a dulled spirit until they experience a moment of heightened clarity in a risky situation—on a mountain, or elsewhere. Then they realize they have the possibility to participate in their own lives with an intensity they could not previously imagine. They understand part of the meaning of what it is to be a "fully functioning person." Abraham Maslow called such experiences "self-actualization." People feel more unified and whole at such moments, more at the creating center of their lives. They are reminded that they can grow beyond perceived comfort zones.

"Why climb mountains?" is a question which, it turns out, cannot be fully answered even by mountain climbers. Everyone attempts an answer. But all freely admit the whole truth is not there.

Why do people seek meaning and purpose? The truth is not always clear here, either. We do know that to understand something with our minds doesn't necessarily mean we will feel it with our hearts or live it. All the best books on gardening will not make a flower grow. Someone goes into the soil, takes a seed and plants it, and gives it the nourishment it needs. The road to purpose is the same. It necessitates that we find in our daily lives ways to risk new attitudes toward life and work. Purpose means taking new risks! Risk is the element in life everyone wishes would go away! All risk involves elements of uncertainty. Activities involving risk require full concentration on the action being performed.

To go risk-free in detecting and living a life purpose is

not possible, because the only kinds of situations that offer certainty and predictability don't make any difference. You might as well get used to the idea that risk rides with you wherever you go.

Conventional wisdom persuades us that intelligent people avoid risks: "An ounce of prevention...", "Look before you leap." Even the word *risqué*, suggests off-base behavior, not prudent, out of line.

The idea that life or work can be risk-free, planned, orderly, and predictable is, of course, the grandest form of self-delusion. Risking is the normal state of affairs in all development; it means you are open to opportunities, to changes in yourself, and to new ways of putting your strengths to use.

When does the need to increase your risk-taking become so important you can no longer ignore it?

- *"I'm bored. I need a new challenge."*—When your spirit has withered and nothing pushes you or kindles your sense of exploration? When routine living has dulled your emotions?

- *"I'm trapped. I've stopped growing."*—When you seem to need to confront a natural anxiety about the unknown? Will I have the nerve? Are my skills and knowledge sufficient to meet the demands of a new situation?

- *"I'll want to move eventually, but it's not urgent."*— When you talk a lot about what you're going to do, but do nothing; talking to friends about the same things week after week?

- *"I'm panicked, desperate."*—When a life transition occurs? When kids leave home or graduate; you lose your job; there's another reorganization, etc., etc.?

It's difficult to find a sense of meaning or purpose in our lives if we're feeling rusted-out or burned-out. Willy Loman expressed it in *Death of a Salesman*: "Guts is getting up and going to work every morning."

The ultimate value of risk-taking is that each person

127

confronts existentially the decision as to whether or not to venture forth into the unknown. Choice is exercised, the mind and body committed, and the consequences accepted. Some individuals pursue risks for meaning and purpose; others for love of challenge, for self-testing, exploration, or camaraderie. Many simply seek a change of pace or change of focus in their lives.

Pushing oneself or one's ideals with the possibility of some loss is one definition of risk-taking. The stress encountered while engaging in any kind of risk activity represents a new beginning. For the most dedicated, the challenge arises from within the psyche. Whether or not it requires the development of new skills or the ability to endure physical hardship, the result is the same—a quest for growth; for the extension of human ability. The satisfaction gained from this challenge has been linked by some to a mystical experience and the very essence of life itself. As Eleanor Roosevelt wrote, **"The purpose of life, after all, is to live it, to taste experience to the utmost, to reach out eagerly and without fear for newer and richer experience."**

What emerges in risk situations is our total involvement. Not only are our senses heightened and our emotions aroused, but everything is focused on the successful completion of the experience. We can put our whole self into it. This is not a death wish. It is a life wish. It is an enhancement of our life through testing ourself at the edge of growth. This is a way to live a healthy and satisfying life, to savor the challenges that expand our potential.

In studies of the life satisfaction of many people, the same themes repeat themselves. What most people want out of life, more than anything else, is the opportunity to grow and to make choices.

Choice involves risk. Oscar Wilde said, "An idea that isn't risky is hardly worth calling an idea."

Sooner or later we all realize that the greatest tragedy in life is to stop growing—to not exercise our choices.

Through risk, we gain a perspective on what it means to be alive and to be a human being.

We can find satisfaction in healthy risks if we balance the pleasure of success with a willingness to learn and grow from our failures as well. Rather than approaching a risky experience as something of serious ego-importance, we can look on it with humility, and allow it to teach us about ourselves. We no longer have to fear failure, for we can appreciate that the worst outcome is not failure, but learning something about ourselves!

We all fight and work under some handicap, whether it be mental or physical. Courage to undertake the hard work of finding our best selves, to move our best selves gracefully through everyday problems, is present in all of us.

Helen Keller said, "Life is either a daring adventure or nothing."

For most people it is just that—nothing! Even our daring adventures turn out to be nothing. It seems that "we don't make a difference."

People who feel as if they don't make a difference aren't big enough to shoulder the responsibility of taking a stand— of risking to care.

Take a look at what you're doing with **your** life.

Take a look at what your friends are doing with **their** lives.

Chapter 18

TAKING A STAND

We have come full cycle in our journey through the notion of purpose. As you now realize, there's a lot more to purpose than simply espousing grandiose values. Turning your visions into realities is no easy business. However, it is far from total drudgery, and there is one fantastic payoff—the feeling of aliveness that comes from taking a stand on something you feel strongly about.

The feeling of aliveness is experienced by becoming focused or absorbed in an issue, value, or dream. Then doing the task becomes its own reward. Terry Fox spoke of experiencing an ecstatic joy while "doing" the Marathon of Hope.

Concentration becomes automatic. Time passes faster. The focus creates energy. You feel energized and in control. There are not enough hours in the day.

For some, the greatest joy in life doesn't come from money, prestige or leisure. It comes from experiencing the power of purpose as a result of total immersion in something they believe in.

In one sense, the essence of this book has been to provide you with practical ideas that will enable you to experience the feeling of commitment that comes from the power of purpose.

A basic need of all human beings is to make a positive commitment to our fellow human beings, as well as to grow and enjoy our personal lives. To a great degree, our personal sense of self-worth is a function of how much we are living this commitment. Taking a stand with your life and work, at its best, involves being yourself, completely and naturally, being honest, and choosing something (or many things) that you genuinely love to do, and that your strengths support.

"Until one is committed
there is hesitancy, the chance to draw back,
always ineffectiveness.
Concerning all acts of initiative (and creation),
there is one elementary truth,
the ignorance of which kills countless ideas
and splendid plans:
that the moment one definitely commits oneself,
then Providence moves too.
All sorts of things occur to help one
that would never otherwise have occurred.
A whole stream of events issues from the decision,
raising in one's favour all manner
of unforeseen incidents and meetings
and material assistance
which no man could have dreamt
would have come his way.

I have learned a deep respect
for one of Goethe's couplets:
'Whatever you can do, or dream you can, begin it.
Boldness has genius, power, and magic in it.'"
—W. H. Murray

Probably the hardest part of getting what we want in life is, first, just figuring out what we really want; but, second, to "begin it," to take that first step.

As soon as I have found something clearly worth doing in my life, it begins to evolve almost immediately (often within days of my becoming clear about it). I experience this as a kind of **"blinding glimpse of the obvious" (or B.G.O.)—when I suddenly get a very strong sense of what I want, and an equally strong sense that I'm going to go for it!** It usually takes a certain amount of time and energy processing it before I arrive at that B.G.O. And very often the B.G.O. is preceded by feelings of being in limbo, of hopelessness, confusion, and self-doubt.

The nature of life is growth. Goals give us a focus and direction in which to channel our growth. Goals transform our life principles and purposes into action. Goals are based on the basic life principle that I make a difference.

In order to make a difference, we've got to be able to make commitments in our lives. When we have a commitment to create or accomplish something, we deeply desire it, believe we can do it, and are totally willing to have it. The clearer and stronger the intention, the more quickly and easily the goal will manifest itself, and usually within a very short time.

Goal-setting does not mean we have to suffer. Goals can be made in the spirit that life is a "mystery to be lived" or a "game to be played."

Many of us go through life not clear about what we want, but pretty sure this isn't it! Relatively few people have set well defined, realistic, and rewarding goals for themselves. Probably ninety out of a hundred people live their present lives reactively, as it unfolds, with little of their behavior aimed at bringing about long-term results.

Yet everyone has **dreams.** Our dreams or visions for our lives come in varying degrees of intensity and priority. The priorities shift and change with events in our lifetime, and with movement from one stage of life to another.

An ancient philosopher said, "Age puts more wrinkles in the mind than in the face." Although there is no law that we must become more rigid, narrow, and resistant to change and commitment, this seems to happen to a majority of us as we grow older. We learn to not care so much; to not take a stand. Why? Why do we tend to set our values and opinions in concrete and settle down to the comfortable routines that we follow for the rest of our lives?

Relatively few people maintain a conscious principle of taking a stand—continuing to learn new things, setting new goals, and becoming more awake in various areas. Purpose and goal-setting go hand in hand.

I have observed that purpose-full people organize their lives around learning experiences and opportunities to try new and different things. They consciously include activities in their lives which challenge them and bring out strengths and talents they never knew they had. They consciously reflect on their touchstone values and principles and keep organizing and reorganizing their lives so as to live those values as much as possible. They take responsibility for making their lives interesting and making their lives make a difference. It seems to come down to this basic, observable truth: **Life is either hard and satisfying or easy and unsatisfying.**

By setting goals, making plans, and taking risks to achieve them, we can consciously avoid "wrinkles of the mind," otherwise known as "psychosclerosis" ("hardening of the categories"). Anthropologist Ashley Montague coined this term to refer to the psychological aging process. That choice includes a preoccupation with routine and comfort, a progressively rigid frame of mind, dominated by fixed opinions and value judgments and less willingness to take risks.

Since we generally feel happiest when we have something to look forward to, it makes sense to always have something to look forward to.

Since dreams affect our motivation, how we do things, what is important to us in life, and our future decisions, it is important to explore our dreams. Clarifying our dreams and goals helps develop our ability to make decisions about future direction. Through the discovery of goals we can learn what we want, and their order of importance. Goals give direction and order to our energies.

No matter who you are you get just 168 hours a week. You can't buy more. You can't stage a sit-down strike for more. You can't negotiate for more. So you have a choice. You can let your life just sort of happen and watch it disappear in the name of being spontaneous. Or you have another choice. You can turn your dreams into goals. You can learn to spend your time wisely—as if it really were money and you wanted to get the most for your buck.

What you get in return is satisfaction. Now. Today. And in the future.

Mark Twain observed that "Habit is habit, and not to be thrown out of the window by any man, but coaxed downstairs a step at a time." This advice actually gives you all you need to know about goal-setting.

If you take Mark Twain's prescription seriously, you must make a planned program of coaxing your goals down the stairs one step at a time. In coaxing your goals, keep in mind these general rules:

1. <u>Start with plenty of possibilities</u>; complete the dream list on the next page. Create at least one goal in each key result area: Choose only those goals **you** really value.

2. <u>Prioritize the possibilities</u>; give priority to the key areas in most need of development; consider how your priorities fit in with your sense of purpose and your touchstone values.

3. <u>Pick one or two to work on</u>; start small at first; choose a combination of a short-range (six-month) and a long-range (three-year) goal.

4. <u>Subdivide both the short- and long-range goals</u> into manageable action steps ("to be . . . coaxed downstairs a step at a time").

5. <u>Do some immediate information gathering</u>; avoid the "New Year's resolution" syndrome; clarify or eliminate vague or overly general goals; make them concrete by gathering face-to-face information from resources around you.

6. <u>Write down the goals</u>; date them; keep them brief and in a place where you can frequently review them.

7. <u>Choose a goal partner</u> to help you monitor and keep your commitments; select benchmark dates to review your progress.

8. <u>Celebrate completion</u> of your goal; make the process fun.

Goals are statements of measurable results to be achieved. Goals help you in translating purpose and dreams into reality. We accept the use of goals in many areas of life (e.g., shooting par in golf, traveling to see the pyramids, running in a 10Km race, living in the Rocky Mountains, having a greenhouse, etc.)

Most of us have more choice about what happens in our lives than we believe. **People step aside for a person with a plan** (perhaps because there are so few of them!). When was the last time you tried to write down or prioritize your goals?

REFLECTION #22

LIFE DREAMS AND PRIORITIES

Take fifteen minutes and write below all the things you can think of that you'd like to experience, explore, achieve, have, do or be, etc. during your lifetime. Put them in words that make sense to you. Start with simple, obvious things.

Personal (health, travel, hobbies, personal growth, adventure, etc.)

Work (career growth/change, earnings, new skills, second income, credentials, early retirement, etc.)

Relationships (family activities, marriage enrichment, new friendships, etc.)

(continued)

Purpose (spiritual growth, community service projects, church activities, problems you're interested in solving, people you're interested in helping, etc.)

Lifestyle (housing alternatives, geographic locale, second home, complexity or simplicity of living, life balance, etc.)

Others:

Now put an A next to the priorities that you would like to take some action on or make a commitment to in the **next twelve months**! Then circle the one that feels like it has the "most" interest or urgency for you to begin working on **today**!

Only when goals are translated into priorities can satisfying results be achieved. To get somewhere, we must know three things:

- Where we are going.
- How we expect to get there.
- When we expect to arrive.

Since none of us has the time and resources to do all of the things we want to do, we make choices based on our value systems—what we want and expect out of life and work.

Sharing your purpose and priorities with someone is an

important part of commitment. Other people can provide support and different points of view—and sharing your goals can be a way by which others become committed to some kind of purposeful action. This can also be an important aid to keeping yourself on track.

REFLECTION #23

Take your circled goal and make a commitment to it. Break it down into specific steps. "Coax [it] downstairs a step at a time." Ask yourself, "What do I need that I don't now have?"

Also, please place a copy of this letter in a sealed envelope **addressed to yourself** and give to your goal partner to be mailed back to you in two months. This will remind you of what actions you have taken and what level of commitment is still present.

_____
(date)

Dear_____

I have just completed reading a book entitled *The Power of Purpose*. The book is about "making a difference" in life, through our choices and commitments. I have decided that an important commitment for me to make is to

_____
_____
_____
_____
_____

I have decided to complete this project by
_____, and plan to take these steps:
           (date)

- By_____I will have_____.
- By_____I will have_____.
- By_____I will have_____.
- By_____I will have_____.
- By_____I will have_____.

(continued)

I would like your help in monitoring my progress.
Would you meet with me on_____and_____so
                          (date)   (date)
I can share my progress with you.

_____
_____
_____
_____

Thanks for your support.
Sincerely,

_____
(your name)

- Who can be of help in further developing my purpose?
- Who will be affected by my commitment?
- Who can influence the success of my goals?

Questions like these can help you identify people who can be goal partners. People around you can be catalysts, prodders, listeners, and sources of helpful information. These people are your purpose network.

Chances are that the goal-setting process will be more realistic and satisfying for you if you involve your network. Most of us need someone to talk to, share feelings with, ask advice of, react to. But for each of us, these people will be different.

Develop a list of people who can provide you with honest feedback in relation to your values, principles, purpose, and goals.

How many of these people do you need? That's up to you. It is important, however, that they:

- Ask good questions and challenge you to think.
- Listen effectively.
- Provide you with realistic information.
- Support your right to make your own decisions. (They don't expect you to be just like they are.)

REFLECTION #24

List the names of people you consider part of your network; people whose opinions you respect, whom you consider supportive, with whom you feel comfortable sharing deep ideas, or who are important sources of information regarding your commitments.

PURPOSE NETWORK

1. Family or friends I can call on or visit for support.
   - _____
   - _____
   - _____
   - _____
   - _____
   - _____

2. People I know in my work who can serve as advisors or sounding boards for my plans.
   - _____
   - _____
   - _____
   - _____
   - _____
   - _____

3. Other resources available to me (professional colleagues, counselors, clergy, church or community groups, etc.).
   - _____
   - _____
   - _____
   - _____
   - _____
   - _____

4. People who might hinder my plans.
   - _____
   - _____
   - _____
   - _____
   - _____
   - _____

"I learned long ago," said Peter Drucker, author and management consultant, "that the most serious mistakes are not being made as a result of wrong answers. The truly dangerous thing is asking the wrong questions."

This is where your network can help most—by asking the right questions at the right time in the right way!

Try the following suggestions to involve your network in this process. **Don't just read this book, use it!**

- Start a journal to keep track of the ups and downs of your search for a purpose.
- Share your insights with a special friend. Involve him or her in discussing an exercise or two.
- Create a study group. Locate several other people who are interested in discussing questions like those in this book. Discuss one section or chapter at each session. Support each other's progress and ideas.
- Attend professional meetings. Risk discussing "purpose" with your professional colleagues.
- Plan a "get-away weekend" to discuss purpose and priorities.
- Gather a group of neighbors to share and learn about your individual directions and struggles.

Through setting up a step-by-step program of action, you have committed yourself to at least one highly specific short-term goal that will help you clarify your long-haul purpose and direction. The process is ultimately to help you enjoy your life more and make a difference.

Commitments do not come easily. Time, effort, and patience are required. One of the prices you may have to pay is letting go somewhere else. You'll probably have to rearrange your priorities and to sacrifice somewhere. What might you have to give up in order to invest more deeply in your goal or purpose? It can be unnerving to see not only what you can do, but what you have to go through to do it! Once goals are committed to and communicated, there is no place to hide. That's why many of us avoid goals—to avoid taking responsibility for our lives!

Chapter 19

PURPOSEFUL REFLECTION: SOLOING AND JOURNALING

It's only as one turns toward solitude that the truth becomes apparent. Periodically we need to give ourselves time and to sit quietly and let our core catch up to us, to listen to the still, small voice inside. Do you provide time in your day for reflection? How satisfied are you with the quality of that time?

To reach under the surface of things, we need to pay genuine attention to all that's there. Discovering a sense of purpose through the workday routine of job, family, etc., is not easy. Our daily routine often lacks any sense of "what for?" Life sometimes appears to have no purpose, to serve no apparent ends.

Great is the need in my own life for deliberate reminders of the "what for?" Yet I'm shocked when I realize how little most of us practice daily reflection. Through purposeful reflection, we see beyond the limits. We know not with the mind but with the heart. Our reflective side recognizes a power beyond the natural and rational and accepts the unknown on faith.

How about you? Do you consider yourself to be a reflective person?

There are steps you can take to enhance your "reflectiveness" and consequently your overall purpose-fullness.

141

The process of reflection is an experience that creates perspective and gives us energy. When we get out of touch with what's primary in life—our touchstone values—we lose our life energy. We gain back our energy and vitality in renewing our touchstones—and by letting them once again guide our day-to-day decisions.

At times we are receptive to reflection; at other times, we are not. At times crises drop into our lives and we are forced to reflect—to deal with the "Who am I?" and "What for?" questions. At other times we don't sense the need at all. Our reflective skills rust silently from lack of use.

How can you stay in touch with the meaning of your life and regularly address your purpose?

The Daily Solo

A major element of purposeful reflection is to plan a fifteen-minute "time out" each day in order to be quiet and not be distracted by your busyness. The more regularly you take this "time out" (called a **solo**), the more you start unmasking illusions. Slowly you'll start discerning what parts of your busyness are an expression of your real values. Achieving a clearer vision requires a few moments daily. Reflection is, for many of us, as tough as it is inevitable. A solo can help you manage your life more effectively on a day-to-day basis. Soloing is simply a process of focusing your priorities, feelings, and thoughts on a regular basis.

"How do I take a daily **solo**?"

First of all, sit down! In the morning, for instance, get up a little earlier, and before you get involved in anything, just sit quietly and for three to four minutes pay full attention to your thoughts and feelings.

Then focus your thoughts. You might imagine yourself feeling calm and peaceful, or perhaps having a great relationship (e.g., really listening to someone that day). Or you might picture yourself moving through the day living a particular value or purpose. You can work on any level and

142

all will bring results. An architect first has an idea or a plan, then designs a building. An artist often has a similar inspiration. Think of your **solo** as time to create a blueprint for your life and purpose.

Repeat this solo often; **at least once per day.** Some people are more inclined to take a solo in the middle or at the end of the day, others, during a lunch break. Some just go to a quiet place or sit down in the office and unplug the phone. Others take their solo just before they come home from work or just before they go to bed.

Ideally, we should not let a day pass without spending some solo time nurturing the spiritual in us. Eventually we really start listening to our deepest selves; and there is an enormous hunger for that. The solo is a daily reminder of our deepest, most basic attitudes toward life.

REFLECTION #25

Step 1: Relaxing

Try this ten-minute solo exercise. Relaxation plays an important role in reflection. In a relaxed state, you will find it easier to concentrate your attention in the direction you choose and to develop a much clearer perception of the events in your life.

- Sit in a comfortable position. Consciously examine your physical tension and describe it to yourself in detail. Examine its intensity. Become as aware as you possibly can of the tension and related discomfort. Tighten up the area; then relax it. If you touch the tense area with your hand, you will feel the discomfort. Interesting areas to try are your jaw, back, neck, and eye muscles. Most people are tense in these areas without being fully aware of it.

- Close your eyes. Take several slow, deep breaths, breathing from your abdomen. Breathe in and out through your nose, taking breaths that are long and slow. Silently count "one" as you inhale and "two" as

(continued)

---

you exhale. Do this over and over again for several minutes. Concentrate on the numbers one and two, saying them to yourself for each breathing cycle. (The idea here is to clear your mind. Most of us feel controlled by thoughts that constantly pop into our minds. Visualize your thoughts as clouds floating toward you, floating freely into your mind, and then floating out of your mind again. Keep going back to counting your breaths. It will become easier as you practice.)

Step 2: Focusing

• After you've enjoyed yourself in the quiet for several minutes, think of something you would like. Picture a principle or value which you would like to live this day, or some behavior in your life which you'd like to improve.

• Spend another three to four minutes picturing yourself there and everything happening just as you want it. What are you doing? What are people saying? What are you feeling? What purposes or values are you trying to live? Don't worry if you don't actually see a picture in your mind. Some people do, but others feel that they don't really "see" anything; they just think about it or have a "feeling" impression. That will do just fine. Have fun with it.

• Keeping the picture in your mind, affirm silently to yourself: "All things are now working together for this (purpose, value) in my life." To affirm means to "make firm" that which you are picturing. If doubts or contradictory thoughts arise, don't resist them. Just let them flow through your mind, and return to your images.

• Don't be in a big hurry to open your eyes. Before you do, suggest to yourself that you are getting more and more alert—that you will feel clear and calm when you return.

As you see, the "solo" process is relatively simple. Using it really effectively, however, usually requires consistent daily practice.

If you are sincere in your intention and open to change, you will soon find that the solo experience will become easier and more flowing and you will look forward to being by yourself. "What we brood over—hatches out!" What this means from a practical standpoint is that we always attract into our lives whatever we think about the most, believe in most strongly, or expect on the deepest levels. Try it for a week with an open mind and heart, and then judge for yourself whether it is useful to you.

If so, continue using and developing the solo habit, and soon the changes in yourself and your sense of purpose will become an integral part of your day. It becomes a continuous awareness, a state of "mindfulness." The solo (with visualization) is one of the most powerful tools you have at your disposal. Your mind and the images within it determine the success or failure of your goals and purpose.

Journal

Most of us are aware of the fact that we have a nearly continuous "inner conversation" going on in our minds. The mind is always talking to itself, keeping up a perpetual commentary about life, feelings, fears, joys, other people, etc. This inner conversation influences our thoughts and feelings about what's going on in our lives, and it is this commentary that creates everything that happens to us. Anyone who has tried to quiet this inner conversation long enough to connect with his deeper, wiser, intuitive mind, knows how difficult it is.

"Journaling" helps us to become aware of the types of thoughts that we habitually think. It helps us to observe our inner conversation more objectively.

Our mind is like a tape recorder. Many of our thoughts are old tapes we've had all our lives (e.g., the "clean-plate club", "promise you'll always do your best . . .", etc.). The old tapes still influence what's happening to us today.

Journaling helps us to begin replacing our worn-out or unwanted tapes with conscious ideas and visions.

A journal can serve as your **purpose workbook**. The following pages have thirty days of journal space to let you try it out.

There are many creative ways to use a journal, such as:

- Recording your thoughts or insights after reading inspiring and uplifting books that keep you in touch with your highest values and purposes.
- Recording or clarifying goals and dreams.
- Collecting quotes, pictures, poems, etc. that are meaningful and inspiring to you.
- Using your journal as a scrapbook for creative ideas.
- Using your journal as a road map of your search for purpose.

Your journal is a good listener. It is a tool for self-guidance, a mirror of your inner conversations. It is not a book written for other people's eyes. It is a place to be reflective. Style is less important than recording the truth!

You will need to write in the journal regularly until you feel the benefits of the habit. As was once said, "If you wait for inspiration, you're not a writer, but a waiter!"

I keep a journal in which I regularly work on my goals, dreams, and purposes. It helps me awaken my senses and be more honest with myself. It's a road map of my growth.

REFLECTION #26

For each of the next thirty days, respond in writing to the question: "The most meaningful moment for me today was . . . ?" (a mental "souvenir" I'll keep).

Also, each day, jot down any creative ideas, plans, or dreams that come to you.

If you take a few minutes a day (perhaps during your solo time), you will find the quality of your life shifting.

MONDAY _____
Reflections:

TUESDAY _____
Reflections:

WEDNESDAY _____
Reflections:

THURSDAY _____
Reflections:

FRIDAY _____
Reflections:

SATURDAY/SUNDAY _____
Reflections:

MONDAY _____
Reflections:

TUESDAY _____
Reflections:

WEDNESDAY _____
Reflections:

THURSDAY ―――――――
Reflections:

FRIDAY ―――――――
Reflections:

SATURDAY/SUNDAY ―――――――
Reflections:

MONDAY _____
Reflections:

TUESDAY _____
Reflections:

WEDNESDAY _____
Reflections:

THURSDAY _____
Reflections:

FRIDAY _____
Reflections:

SATURDAY/SUNDAY _____
Reflections:

MONDAY _____
Reflections:

TUESDAY _____
Reflections:

WEDNESDAY _____
Reflections:

THURSDAY _____
Reflections:

FRIDAY _____
Reflections:

SATURDAY/SUNDAY _____
Reflections:

Other Strategies for Self-Management

In addition to the daily solo and journal, here is a list of other common-sense strategies for daily self-management. None of these strategies is new, but we often need to be reminded of them. Add your own to the list.

- Have one "to do" list. Cross out tasks as you finish them. Carry undone items forward to a new list. Divide the list into three sections: Vital; Important; Routine. Set deadlines for finishing each task.

- Discover a "hideaway"—a place where you can plan and organize yourself on a regular basis, where you can work on your life priorities.

- Simplify your life! Begin to eliminate unnecessary commitments.

- Practice saying "no" to things you really don't want to do. Read a book on assertiveness if you have trouble doing this in a firm but kind way.

- Set aside a ten-minute block at the end of each day, devoted solely to planning tomorrow—to completing your "to do" list.

- Develop a mental picture of a model week. Allot time for "solo," planning, work, exercise, leisure, family and community activities. Then live with it until it becomes a habit.

- Take time to be with "nutritious" people—people with whom you can be most honest.

- Learn a variety of relaxation techniques and practice at least one regularly.

- Laugh more! Create a humor "first-aid kit." Set a goal for yourself of at least one belly laugh a day.

- Remember to use helpful clichés such as, "Life is not a dress rehearsal!" or "A risk-a-day keeps inner kill away!"

- Take time to be aware of nature. Even in cities, the sky, the breeze, and seasonal changes can add perspective and enhancement.

- Practice "mindfulness"—keeping your mind focused on the present. Do whatever you're doing more slowly, more intentionally—don't waste your precious present.

- Take frequent relaxation breaks. Take deep, slow breaths often, especially while in a meeting, on the phone, or driving your car. Use this time to renew yourself.

- Cultivate the ability to enjoy each day! Plan to do something that is pure "fun" each day—something you love to do, something just for you. Set a realistic schedule to include time for spontaneity.

- Celebrate minor anniversaries or triumphs in a big way.

- Give a piece of music your undivided attention.

- Exercise daily.

- Reduce your intake of sugar, salt, caffeine, and alcohol.

- Create and maintain a personal-support network—people who really listen to you and are catalysts for your thinking.

- Plan periodic "getaway weekends" with a spouse or friend—take time to just "care, not cure" anything.

- Get a massage and/or learn to massage your own face, shoulders, and feet.

- Study your daily energy pattern—capitalize on your "golden hours" (your high-energy time)—listen to your inner signals.

- Practice "I" statements. Change "I should" to "I choose to" or "I want."

- Set up a time in your week to handle major problems. Every time the nagging problem begins to bother you, write a note with your thoughts on it and put it in your "problem file." Then at the appointed time, pull out the file and work through the problem, uninterrupted.

- When you read your mail, act on it immediately (e.g., respond to it, toss it, file it).

- Carry a card with your monthly goals and commitments written on it.

- Prioritize your activities daily and focus on the top two each day until they're completed.

- Develop active listening skills. Remember what Voltaire said: "The way to the heart is the ear."

Chapter 20

DARE WE BE OURSELVES?

From early childhood we are taught to behave in ways that are approved by others. As children, we are naturally open, yet dependent on the lead set by others. To follow the lead of our parents, peers, teachers, etc., provides us with security. Sooner or later we realize it is easier to base our behavior on "what is expected of us" rather than on "what is meaningful to us." Sometimes we become so dependent on these "external" standards that we no longer know what we truly feel.

The habit of behaving in an approved manner is comforting because it means that we seldom have to look at our own shortcomings or take responsibility for our own lives.

What value is there in living like this? When we live in a constant approval-seeking mode, our feelings are buried alive. Feelings buried alive, however, live! We are unable to experience pleasure or joy very deeply; suppressing our inner nature blocks the flow of our actions and relationships with others.

We manage to maintain a smooth manner, hiding our true feelings. But though we act as if everything were fine— "How are you?" "Just fine, thank you."—dissatisfaction gradually builds up within us. We become skilled at creating the impression that things are going well.

We wait. We spend much of our life waiting. What a strange hold this waiting has on us. Waiting for a sign. Waiting to be rescued. Not committing ourselves to anything until everything is right. Waiting for the grand opportunity, when our full talents and feelings will be unleashed and used up.

Approval by its very nature traps us in a way of living that makes even our leisure activities superficial and disappointing. We do not know where to turn to find value in life. Because we find so little fulfillment within ourselves, we may look for happiness and self-worth in possessions and social success.

All of us want the best out of life. We want to be healthy and happy and to have things that can enrich our experience. Yet, though we strive for these things, we end up dissatisfied. We may have a "good" life. But if we do not tap our own inner nature, then a large portion of each day is spent doing something we do not truly care about and would rather not be doing. We may spend so much of our lives seeking approval that we never awaken to the joy of real living. Life will end. Death will claim us—and we will not have had more than a moment of contentment.

"Being ourselves" is probably the most personal and most difficult issue we can address because it involves looking inward and requires reflection, which is a frightening prospect for many people. And it is not something another person can do for us, because reflection is a **process.**

One of the requirements of that process is making friends with death rather than running from it. Living well and experiencing life fully means facing squarely the question of death.

Death can be a highly creative force. The highest values of life can originate from brushing up against it.

Squarely facing our own mortality lets us take a fresh approach, ditch all the traditional gambits and start from scratch. It shatters some attitudes—"But what can I do?"—and generates aliveness.

An awareness of our own mortality alerts us to the question, "What holds me back from fully experiencing my life?"

Many people claim they don't fear death. But, death has many images.

"It's not that I'm afraid of dying; I just don't want to be there when it happens."

—Woody Allen

"The fear of death is the basic fear that influences all others; a fear from which no one is immune no matter how disguised it may be."

—Ernest Becker

"When a man knows he is to be hanged in a fortnight, it concentrates his mind wonderfully."

—Samuel Johnson

"The confronting of death gives the most positive reality to life itself. It makes the individual existence real, absolute, and concrete. Death is the one fact of my life which is not relative but absolute and my awareness of this gives my existence and what I do each hour an absolute quality."

—Rollo May

Few people express no anxiety about death. What do you fear about death? In the *Art of Dying* by Robert F. Neale, the fears of death are listed in three categories. What do you fear about death? Have a dialogue with yourself about each of the fears.

1. *Fear of what happens after death.*
   - Fate of my body—idea that my physical body will decay
   - The unknown that follows—the unendingness of eternity

2. *Fear of the process of dying.*
   - The pain—the final struggle
   - Indignity—the humiliation of giving up control of bodily functions
   - Being a burden—few of us will die by accident; becoming a physical, emotional or financial burden

3. *Fear of the loss of life*.
   - Loss of mastery—end of our control over life
   - Incompleteness and failure—not tasting, experiencing, learning, achieving all we intended to
   - Separation—being taken from those we love; sorrow and hardship to family and friends

Which fears best describe your situation? To face death consciously is to face life consciously. How do your fears (above) reflect upon the ways you live your life now?

REFLECTION #27

Reflect on the following questions. Discuss them with someone close to you.

1. The thing that has surprised me most about this stage of my life is . . .

2. When I think about my own death, the greatest fear I have is (review the list above) . . .

3. What will be important to you at the moment of your death? What will it take by way of achievements or feelings or things, for you to die satisfied? Sit back for a few minutes to reflect on this. Jot down your thoughts below. Your response will provide an orientation for living!

Whenever we take a new risk, we may find ourselves attending to the negatives—the obstacles that might arise. We are constrained by an underlying sense of fear—of not measuring up. This fear hinders the free flow of our strengths. Because we are afraid to commit all our energy, we begin to undermine our power of purpose.

We look for the easy way out. We put our energy into rationalizing and finding excuses rather than into the task itself. Our attention wanders. Our motivation wavers. Our enjoyment is gone. When we fail to commit our talents and energy fully, we find it difficult to take responsibility for the results of our life and work.

But honesty is worth the effort. When we are honest with ourselves and others, there is a clarity in all our actions. We develop our inner nature and our awareness leads to a new and clear perspective.

There is no secret to discovering the quality of our inner natures, for our minds are eager to tell us all about ourselves. All we need to do is listen. We can challenge the approval-seeking behavior that we bring to our life and work by practicing the **solo** and **journaling** techniques in the last chapter. We lead approval-bound lives only because we choose to ignore our own inner signals.

Dare we be ourselves? When?

THE
PURPOSE
CONNECTION

Chapter 21

BLINDING GLIMPSES
OF THE OBVIOUS

Perhaps our purpose in life is to **make a difference.** In some way, each of us has talents and energies to offer to the productive process. Self-esteem is the basis of our ability to accomplish purposeful goals. Acceptance of ourselves, as we are right now, is the basis of healthy self-esteem. This feeling of self-worth is the key to being of worth to others.

Our real satisfaction in life will depend on the quality of contribution we make. Purpose-full people have clearly defined visions which they review regularly. They live on purpose. Leo Buscaglia summed it up nicely:

> **"Each act makes us manifest. It is what we do, rather than what we feel, or say we do that reflects who and what we truly are. Each of our acts makes a statement as to our purpose. Whatever immortality there is, is assured by a continual participation in the productive process. Because of us, things have become more. Something has been left of significance because we existed."**

Life success favors the bold. "Lucky" people do something to bring about a desired result. They keep their antennae attuned to fresh ideas; they listen to people; they listen to their intuition; they do their homework and go after it.

Successful people respect their hunches—their "blinding glimpses of the obvious." They listen to their intuition and trust their feelings, even if others are skeptical. They acknowledge serendipity. Instead of regarding a crisis or an accident as irrelevant, they look for the possibility that it may present an opportunity. They don't fall into the justice trap—expecting life to be fair. They take off the blinders about the way things "should" happen. **When someone hands them a lemon, they make lemonade!**

Organizations, like individuals, need a reason for being. Peter Drucker argues convincingly that the key question every company must put to itself periodically is: What business are we in? Every leader and manager is eventually haunted by the same question.

Certainly the ultimate goal of any business is to survive and grow.

If you ask a business executive what the purpose of business is you probably will be told "to make a profit," "to provide jobs," etc.

But if we are to increase productivity in this country, business needs another reason for being; it needs to serve people and society in a very special way—to make a real difference in the lives of all who are influenced by it.

A sense of purpose accompanies greatness in anything and is largely responsible for the quality products and services and high morale found in very successful companies. The fact is that those who take the idea of purpose most seriously are the leaders and managers in this country's most successful companies.

As pointed out throughout this book, **purpose** is one of the most important criteria we as individuals have for choosing what to do with our lives. Purpose is the act of consciously applying our motivated strengths and resources to people and projects that move us and in which we believe.

Many organizations are also rediscovering the connection between values, behavior, and productivity. They are making the connection between spirit and work. Their leaders are observing, as Studs Terkel did, "most people have work that is too small for their spirits."

Many once successful companies have gone under because they became so involved in markets, competition, pricing, etc., that they lost sight of their purpose—their reason for being. They forgot to keep asking, "What business are we in?" and "How are the lives of our customers and employees upgraded because of our product or service?"

A company that provides products and services without a purposeful desire to serve has a very good chance of failing. More than eight out of ten new businesses don't even last three years!

Most highly successful organizations do operate "on purpose." As John Naisbitt pointed out in *Megatrends*, "The extraordinarily successful strategic vision of NASA was 'to put a man on the moon by the end of the decade.' That strategic vision gave magnetic direction to the entire organization. Nobody had to be told or reminded of where the organization was going."

Purpose enables people to clarify and realize what they really want, regardless of what presently appears possible. Purpose generates excitement and unifies an organization. Purpose evolves into a clear image of what our reason for being is, which then translates into concrete goals, which then helps individuals to discover their personal "fit." A good "fit" or alignment of personal and organizational purpose is a prerequisite for both commitment and satisfaction.

The viewpoint of this book reflects a deep belief that commitment and personal satisfaction lie not in material rewards alone, but in the opportunity to pursue a vision— to make a difference. Working—**on purpose**—is simply a superior way to do business. It means clearly and honestly deciding and communicating what business we are in, and focusing our collective energies accordingly. The questions we ask in determining organizational purpose are the very same ones that effective and purposeful individuals ask:

Who are we?

Why are we here?

What are our motivated strengths?

What do we have to contribute which is unique or different?

What special technology or knowledge do we have?

What do we value?

What needs are we moved to meet?

Organizations with leaders, managers, and employees who regularly ask such questions discover that new products, services and ways of doing business often evolve and that the core personal values people wish to have in their work are satisfied.

The answers to these questions tell us more about our purpose—our reason for being. The result is a statement of the mission of the organization, along with the values and commitments that drive it.

From this point of view, then, strategic planning becomes a search for a new purpose or a recommitment to the existing purpose. The exercise becomes one of forging a shared view of our intentions which will serve as our guide in day-to-day decision-making.

Adopting such a point of view requires a fundamental leap in our orientation to work. At first glance, purpose is not an idea likely to appeal to most hardheaded business people. Yet the "power of purpose" has actually been around for a long, long time.

Studies of high-performing athletes consistently turn up findings which suggest this notion. Successful athletes are prone to create a clear and conscious long-term intention to guide their short-term, day-to-day training activities.

Successful innovators and leaders in almost all fields are prone to envision the results they want.

Peters and Waterman in the all-time, best-selling business book, *In Search of Excellence*, found that top executives of excellent companies ensure that no corporate decision affecting internal or external practices goes against the company's purpose. Perhaps they realize the fact that it takes very few lapses in company purpose for internal integrity to be lost.

Excellent companies understand the value of purpose and emphasize its importance in company policies and practices. *In Search of Excellence* confirms that a purpose-driven business organization is not only conceivable, but also desirable in financial and human terms. The book highlights examples of seventy-five very successful American companies which were judged excellent according to various financial and other measures. In these companies, a primary role of executive leadership is to articulate meaning and vision for employees and to create an environment of clear intent. Leaders of excellent companies understand that we really can't compel people to do anything. We can only encourage them to want to do things. They understand that real commitment does not come through autocratic power, but through the power of purpose and caring. In such companies, leaders go far beyond "what's expected" in business life to care for employees and to serve the larger communities surrounding the business. Every organization of value that shows successful growth and profit and makes significant contributions to its field needs the very kind of person it's least likely to accept. Every organization needs a few "cutting edge" people who question where they are going, who challenge the old visions and offer new ones. How does your organization deal with people who probe and ask pertinent questions? Are they shunted out of the way? Given a raise? Organizations get very uncomfortable and insecure when a new vision is presented—when their methods, their rules, and their beliefs are questioned.

During my ten years as a career and life-planning consultant, I have been continually impressed with the hunger that most employees have for some purpose higher than mere career success, for a vision that somehow makes a difference. They want to know what they are working for. What's the mission? Where are they headed and why? What's their role?

Their hunger is for a leader who is a source of vision and vitality and who can articulate a common purpose by which they can work. They hunger for leadership that is guided by strongly held purpose, and who is willing to live that vision. This is the hunger for integrity. Integrity means "living and working on purpose." Purpose is something you do every day. It's not something in an annual report or on a plaque in the reception area—it's to be acted out.

One dictionary definition of integrity is "moral soundness; honesty, freedom from corrupting influences..." The concept of integrity is made clear by thinking about your friends who honestly "live their values" and by comparing them to friends who don't. When we deal with honest friends we have a high level of trust that their promises and values will be lived. Less honest people make statements that are vague, unclear or confusing. Though people may intend to live up to their word, their words must be compared to their actions.

We compare what leaders and companies say their mission and values are with what they do; we compare what they say with their behavior toward their employees and customers.

An organization with integrity is one for which we know that the visions, statements, and promises we hear are accurate.

Purpose in organizations is more difficult to evaluate than individual purpose. We can compare the statements of our friends with their actions. In order to evaluate purpose in an organization, however, we need to compare the collective intent of the leadership with its actions.

I am optimistic about the possibility of introducing "the power of purpose" thinking into organizations. The stimulus and the ingredients now exist for a shift in thinking. John Gardner has summed it up this way:

"Today we can't afford not to take chances—I'm always puzzled by people who talk as though advocates of change are just inventing ways to disturb the peace in what would otherwise be a tranquil community. We are not seeking change for the pure fun of it. We must change to meet the challenge of altered circumstances. Change will occur whether we like it or not. It will either be change in a good and healthy direction or change in a bad and regrettable direction. There is no tranquility for us."

People know that there is something missing, that there should be more to working life than this. The personal needs are there. There is a hunger for purpose. There is an energy waiting to be tapped. They know that change is coming. Yet they cling to the past without really believing in it— "waiting—and distracting themselves with their own careerism.

Purpose is the name for what is missing. In developing a purpose one has to come to terms with the spirit in organizations. Spirituality is an aspect of our existence which is not discussable in most organizations. Yet why do so many people in leadership positions go to churches and synagogues or otherwise ponder the meaning of the circumstances they find themselves in? What goes on in their heads as they ponder the great questions: "Who am I? Why am I here? What am I to do with my life? How do I know that what I am doing is the right thing to do?"

People empowered by a sense of purpose are enthusiastic about the possibility their life holds for making a difference. The original Greek word enthusiasm meant "to be filled with God." When we are "filled with God" we tend to be awake and creatively alive. Organizations today desperately need people who have enthusiasm, whatever the nature of their inspiration. A key is to create an organizational culture in which purpose and mutual caring are the norms.

We are living in an age when America's best companies are discussing and rediscovering the spirit upon which their corporate cultures were built. Many of their leaders recognize the connection between values, behavior and productivity. They are making the connection between our spirit and our work, and will benefit from the productivity unleashed through the power of purpose.

Chapter 22

THE SIMPLE TRUTH

Caring is the basis of all purpose. True purpose is an active caring and openness to everything around us, a willingness to do whatever needs to be done. Purpose is not limited to our personal goals, for in a much greater sense, we are responsible for our total experience; for how we relate to the world around us. **Purpose means understanding the true nature and extent of our responsibility as human beings.**

If we are to have a sense of purpose, we need to strengthen our feelings of caring. We often interpret purpose in terms of curing: healing the sick, inventing a solution, giving to the poor, and ministering to or teaching the needy. But the fact is that we often use our actions to shelter us from caring.

Henri J. M. Nouwen clarified this difference:

"What we see, and like to see, is cure and change. But what we do not see and do not want to see is care, the participation in the pain, the solidarity in suffering, the sharing in the experience of brokenness. And still, cure without care is as dehumanizing as a gift given with a cold heart."

To develop care we need the awareness of how things actually are—not how things should be, according to our closely held opinions and beliefs—but how things really are in people's lives. To develop purpose means being aware of the effects of our actions on others, even on the global level, being aware of the honest-to-God truth of people's

172

circumstances. "Telling the truth" allows us to open up to the real needs of the people around us, and to naturally care, rather than cure out of guilt and largess.

We each have the capacity to contribute our caring energy to life—to make a difference—but, many of us are blocking ourselves from doing so.

Once it has been developed, purpose comes naturally. We are not burdened by a sense of duty or obligation—we care because it is the natural, healthy way to be.

REFLECTION #28

Looking to our past can help us develop our capacity for caring. Remember the very last time you responded openly and fully to another person, considering their true needs as your own. You cared (vs. cured). *Jot down the details of that incident here: what you did, how you felt.*

We all have experienced a time when we were so deeply involved in what we were doing that all that mattered was doing it. We were running on "automatic." Petty thoughts and self-interests did not clutter our concern. At these times, we were clear about our goals; our concentration was devoted to the process of accomplishing them. This power of caring is the power behind purpose. It is the greatest gift we have to offer.

When we ask ourselves honestly which people in our lives mean the most to us—are most nutritious—we often find it is those who, instead of **curing** us, have chosen to just **care**.

Henri J. M. Nouwen states:

"Cure without care makes us preoccupied with quick changes, impatient and unwilling to share each oth-

er's burden. And so cure can often become offending instead of liberating. It is therefore not so strange that cure is not seldom refused by people in need. Not only have individuals refused help when they did not sense a real care, but also oppressed minorities have resisted support, and suffering nations have declined medicine and food when they realized that it was better to suffer than to lose self-respect by accepting a gift out of a non-caring hand."

Purpose-full people in our lives have "few plans for our improvement." From experience we know that they're just there with us unconditionally (asking nothing in return). When they listen, they listen. When they help, they help. We know it is for our sake and not their own.

The purpose-full person understands that being present for each other is what really matters; that cure without care is often more harmful than helpful, that what it means to be a human **being** is to "*be*"!

We develop this caring quality and attract it to us by accepting the demands of life and work with a different attitude—choosing to make a difference.

When we choose to **live and work on purpose**, the results express the clarity and depth of our caring, and we feel a rich sense of inner peace which strengthens our confidence in ourselves. The glow we feel stays with us; our life feels meaning-full.

This simple truth is the real power that lends purpose to our lives.

RECOMMENDED READING

The Road Less Traveled by M. Scott Peck (Simon & Schuster, NY, 1978)

Voluntary Simplicity by Duane Elgin (Wm. Morrow & Co., NY, 1981)

The Inventurers: Excursions in Life and Career Renewal, Janet Hagberg and Richard Leider (Addison-Wesley, Reading, MA, Revised, 1983)

The Denial of Death by Ernest Becker (Free Press, NY, 1973)

Man's Search for Meaning by Viktor Frankl (Pocket Books, NY, 1963)

Excellence by John Gardner (Harper & Row, NY, Revised, 1984)

Self-Renewal by John Gardner (Norton, NY, Revised, 1981)

Taking Stock: A Daily Self-Management Journal by Richard Leider and James Harding (Leider-Harding Publishers, Box 8709, Portland, OR, 1981)

Against the Grain by David Maitland (Pilgrim Press, NY, 1981)

If You Don't Know Where You're Going, You'll Probably End Up Somewhere Else by David Campbell (Argus, Niles, IL, 1974)

Hope for the Flowers by Trina Paulus (Paulist Press, NY, 1972)

Good Work by E. F. Schumacher (Harper Colophon, NY, 1979)

Pathfinders by Gail Sheehy (E. P. Dutton, NY, 1976)

The Way of Life by Lao Tsu (New American Library, NY, 1959)

Personhood by Leo Buscaglia (Fawcett Columbine, NY, 1978)

The Unheard Cry for Meaning by Viktor Frankl (Touchstone, NY, 1978)

The Three Boxes of Life by Richard N. Bolles (Ten Speed Press, Berkeley, CA, 1978)

Creative Visualization by Shakti Gawain (Whatever Publishing, Mill Valley, CA, 1978)

Anatomy of an Illness by Norman Cousins (Bantam, NY, 1981)

Blue Highways by William Least Heat Moon (Fawcett Crest, NY, 1982)

Out of Solitude by Henri J. M. Nouwen (Ave Maria Press, Notre Dame, IN 1974)

Fully Human, Fully Alive by John Powell (Argus, Niles, IL, 1976)

American Spirit by Lawrence M. Miller (Wm. Morrow, NY, 1984)

The Art of Dying by Robert E. Neale (Harper & Row, NY, 1973)

The Truth About You by Arthur F. Miller and Ralph T. Mattson (Fleming H. Revel, Old Tappan, NJ, 1977)

In Search of Excellence by Thomas J. Peters and Robert H. Waterman (Harper & Row, NY, 1982)

The Way of the Peaceful Warrior by Dan Millman (H. J. Kramer, Tiburon, CA, 1980)

Wellness Workbook: A Guide to Attaining High Level Wellness by Regina Sara Ryan and John W. Travis (Ten Speed Press, Berkeley, CA, 1981)

LIVING ON PURPOSE

To: Richard J. Leider
    % Power of Purpose
    7101 York Avenue South
    Minneapolis, Minnesota 55435

I thought you would like to know about a purpose that I discovered that makes a difference in my life:

_____
_____
_____
_____
_____

I am having trouble with the following part of *The Power of Purpose* process:

_____
_____
_____
_____
_____

           Name_____
        Address_____
                   _____

The Power of Purpose Training

Reading a book can be very helpful in the pursuit of purpose, and I hope that this book has been useful to you in clarifying yours.

I also realize that it is difficult sometimes to begin to live and work—on purpose—in your day-to-day activities.

Therefore, in order to help you personally handle the questions, decisions, and process that determines purpose, I have created follow-up training programs for you to use either individually or with a larger group.

These follow-up programs utilize the award-winning *The Power of Purpose* film, time-efficient audiotapes, and workbooks. If you wish further information about these materials you may contact:

> Wilson Learning Corporation
> 6950 Washington Avenue South
> Eden Prairie, MN 55344
> (612) 944-2880

If you would like to receive information on *The Power of Purpose* speeches, seminars and/or newsletter you may contact:

> Leider, Inc.
> 7101 York Avenue South
> Minneapolis, MN 55435
> (612) 921- 3334

ABOUT THE AUTHOR

Dick Leider is one of the nation's leading speakers, consultants, and authors on career and life planning.

As President of Leider, Inc., a Minneapolis, MN firm which develops career planning ideas into programs and films, he is a speaker and seminar leader for many leading corporations (e.g., 3M, Control Data, Pillsbury, Aetna).

He is an adventurer and leads adult renewal expeditions to places like Mt. Kilimanjaro and the Serengeti Plains of Africa.

Dick is the co-author of *The Inventurers: Excursions in Life and Career Renewal* and *Taking Stock: A Daily Self-Management Journal*.

MAKING A LIVING *WORK!*

What are your expectations from work—and from life?

Most people don't like their jobs very much.
But all of us hunger for meaning and purpose
both in our work and in our personal lives.
Now a top author, lecturer, and consultant
to Fortune 500 corporations shows you how to
achieve the power of purpose—and become
the happy, successful person you want to be.

- Identify your most motivated talents.
- Use those talents to further the goals
  you care about.
- Create the work environment that fits
  who you are.
- Learn how to take the risks that get
  you what you want.

THE POWER OF PURPOSE is *not* another book
about goal-setting but a hands-on workbook,
complete with self-assessment questionnaires,
checklists, and exercises, where *you*
participate in realizing total satisfaction
in your life and your career.

12840

0

27778 00295

ISBN 0-449-12840-7